INDUSTRIAL ACTIVITY AND
ECONOMIC GEOGRAPHY

Geography

Editor

PROFESSOR W. G. EAST

Professor Emeritus of Geography
in the University of London

INDUSTRIAL ACTIVITY AND ECONOMIC GEOGRAPHY

A STUDY OF THE FORCES BEHIND THE GEOGRAPHICAL LOCATION OF PRODUCTIVE ACTIVITY IN MANUFACTURING INDUSTRY

R. C. Estall
Reader in Geography at the
London School of Economics and Political Science

and

R. Ogilvie Buchanan
Emeritus Professor of Geography in the
University of London

HUTCHINSON UNIVERSITY LIBRARY
LONDON

HUTCHINSON & CO (*Publishers*) LTD
3 Fitzroy Square, London W1

London Melbourne Sydney Auckland
Wellington Johannesburg Cape Town
and agencies throughout the world

First published 1961
Reprinted 1962, 1963, 1964, 1965
Second (revised) edition 1966
Reprinted 1967, 1968, 1969, 1970 (twice), 1972

*The photograph on the cover of the paperback
edition was taken at the Spencer Works, South
Wales, the Strip mills division of the British Steel
Corporation.*

*Printed in Great Britain by offset litho at
Flarepath Printers Ltd., St. Albans, Herts,
and bound by Wm.Brendon & Son Ltd.,
Tiptree, Essex*
ISBN 0 09 061061 x (cased)
0 09 061062 8 (paper)

TO OUR WIVES

CONTENTS

FIGURES

TABLES

EDITORIAL FOREWORD

It is a mark of the complexity of modern geography that, in its attempts to understand and to explain the world as the home of man, it commonly finds itself organised in our universities within the three faculties of Arts, Science and Economics and, further, that it makes progress by means of the so-called systematic studies, of which Economic Geography is one. This aspect of the main subject naturally engages the interest of those geographers who are also in some measure economists, for it is with the science of Economics that Economic Geography is inevitably much concerned. Students of geography as a whole, however, cannot fail to be interested in Economic Geography, for the works of man there studied, like the works of nature itself, are prime differentials of the world's environments.

We are happy that two of our colleagues who are economic geographers undertook to write for students of geography and others this book which springs from their experience as teachers and researchers. Both are holders of the B.Sc. (Economics) degree and proficient alike in geography and economics. Professor R. O. Buchanan, shortly to retire from his Chair in the University of London, first came to this country with the New Zealand forces during the first world war. He returned here later to graduate with first-class Honours at the Joint School of Geography (of King's College and the London School of Economics), and then both to make contributions to economic geography and to teach for a generation students in turn at University College and the Joint School. He has done much to clarify the field and define the methods of a true Economic Geography, and many students in and outside his own university will now benefit by reading his written words. His younger colleague, Dr R. C. Estall, co-author of this book and another first-class Honours graduate of the Joint School, has already established himself as a vigorous contributor in this field—and together they make a strong pair.

The two authors do not attempt to survey the whole field of Economic Geography but focus their attention on what is, beyond doubt, a matter of ever-growing importance—industrial activity. In a world where most of mankind earn their livelihood from farming of one kind or another, it has not passed unnoticed that the higher standards of living are enjoyed by the industrialised nations. This is not to say that highly rewarding industrial development lies available to all late-starters everywhere, or that in industrialisation lies the panacea for countries which suffer from poverty, over-population and under-development. But two encouraging facts are that resources are man-made and that scientific and technological progress is continually enlarging the range of possibilities in the exploitation of man's estate, possibilities which are much less limited by 'natural endowment' than was once thought. Only by studying industry as it is already located, and by discovering the principles which lie behind successful industrial location, can we hope to guide its spread and progress on a planetary scale.

Those of us who teach the younger generation in our universities cannot be unaware of their desire to see knowledge applied for the betterment or alleviation of the lot of the many 'geographically underprivileged'. Such applications cannot be made by pious aspiration but only by hard thought, following close study. If therefore the reader finds some of the pages which follow stiff going, let him nevertheless persist and be grateful that he is offered such clear and authoritative counsel.

S.W.W.
W.G.E.

PREFACE TO SECOND EDITION

The decision to publish this work as a paperback, following the fifth impression of the original book, presented an opportunity for some revision of the text and for the presentation of more up-to-date material and statistics. These alterations, however, in no way alter the argument. While the conditions affecting the location of a given industry can change over time, the proper location decision will still involve the balancing of the variety of elements, discussed here, that cause costs and profits to vary in different geographical locations. In other words, while the facts of a particular case may change, the *principles* remain the same, and are unchanged by changing statistical situations. The second edition thus follows closely the pattern of the first.

We wish to acknowledge again with our thanks the services of Mrs E. Wilson in re-drawing the maps.

R.C.E.
R.O.B.

1965

PREFACE TO FIRST EDITION

This book, small, introductory and elementary though it is, nevertheless ranges widely, and it will be clear that little of it can be the result of first-hand investigation by the authors themselves of the bewildering array of problems posed by the location of manufacturing industry. It represents rather an attempt to make available to students in concise form material culled from a review of a very extensive literature. It has grown naturally out of the special interest of the Department of Geography in the London School of Economics in the problem of industrial location, and owes much to our colleagues there. In particular we wish to acknowledge the inspiration of Professor M. J. Wise, whose authority in this field needs no labouring. Both he and Dr J. E. Martin have in addition read the manuscript and given us valuable criticisms and suggestions. It must be emphasised, however, that no responsibility rests on their shoulders for any of the shortcomings of the book. The selection and arrangement of material, the balancing of emphasis and the precise form of exposition are our own, and we must accept the responsibility.

It is a great pleasure to acknowledge also our debt to Miss Denise Mechin, who coped most cheerfully and successfully with an arduous job of typing, and to Mrs E. Wilson, who transformed our rough sketches into admirably finished maps.

R.C.E.
R.O.B.

1961

I

SOME PRELIMINARY CONSIDERATIONS

This little book is intended to be a first approach to an understanding of the conditions that affect the *location* of industrial activity, or in other words an introduction to the economic geography of manufacturing industry. This is, it need hardly be said, only one facet of economic geography, which as a whole is concerned with any activity that earns an income in money or in kind, and of which the geography of agriculture, of mining and of transport will readily be recognised as other major fields. The special concern of the economic geographer is with the spatial distributions of productive activities; his task is to establish and to analyse the areal patterns of these distributions, and to arrive, if possible, at valid explanations of them. In this work, however, as befits an introductory essay of limited size, our aim is less ambitious. We are making no attempt to provide a comprehensive economic geography of manufacturing industry. Our purpose is rather to separate and examine the forces that play a part in determining its location. Only if the interplay of these forces is understood can valid thinking on the location of industry result, and the greater part of the book is therefore devoted to a discussion of their nature and operation. The studies of specific industries are included to serve merely as samples of the application of the basic ideas and the methods of reasoning in differing situations.

Even with these limitations of scope and purpose we have on our hands a problem of great complexity. The number of industries is very great, and precisely which considerations are of prime importance for wise location may be different for every one of them. Nor are the requirements always the same even within one single industry: from one country or region to another differences in such things as available techniques, labour conditions, size and organisation of the individual firms, general economic and social environment may induce corresponding differences in the requirements for good location. Nevertheless, however wide these differences may be, there is in every case a combination of influences of which account must be taken if a good choice of location is to be made. The optimum location implies that a balance has been achieved among these influences so that they mesh smoothly and each makes its due contribution to providing the most economic conditions for production.

At this point it must be admitted that not every manufacturer in seeking a location for a new works makes a thorough investigation of all relevant conditions before coming to his decision, and instances are often quoted of decisions being influenced by such matters as the proximity of an attractive golf course for the manufacturer himself or the preference of his wife for one area over another as a place to live in. Such instances have given rise to much loose thinking on the subject of location, and it may be well to try to put them into proper perspective. Important as location is, it seldom happens that only one location will do. For a given enterprise two or more locations, each with a different combination of advantages, may be equally suitable. So, where the final choice is between two such areas, it may be quite reasonable to let the decision be influenced by such preferences of personal taste as were mentioned above. This does, however, imply that the strictly industrial advantages of the two possible areas have first been assessed and shown no marked superiority for either. An entrepreneur who lets his business judgment be swayed *solely* by the sort of golf he wants to play or the sort of social facilities his wife demands is backing himself against all the odds to be lucky enough to hit on a suitable location without having considered its business possibilities. In the exceptional case his luck may hold (after all, outsiders do sometimes win!), but business men of this kind are not likely to remain in business very long. Moreover, it must be noted that the choice of location nowadays often rests, not in the hands of individual entrepreneurs, but in those of the boards of large incorporated companies; while the influence of governments in this field has also tended to increase. It is true, of course, that even in these circumstances non-economic criteria may influence decisions (especially, perhaps, those made by governments) but it is very unlikely that trivial personal considerations will.

If we leave for a moment the problem of what induces the entrepreneur to make the decision he does about the location of his enterprise, the inescapable fact in the present industrial world is the existence of well-marked areas of concentrated industry, some of which have survived for a very long time. All the industries and all the firms in every industry owed their existence in the first place to individual decisions, and the existence of these highly industrialised areas epitomises the consensus of the views and experience of innumerable individuals that these areas had advantages for these industries over other possible areas. For an area, as for an individual, unsuitability to the work to be done makes it difficult to remain in business in a competitive world, and for an area, as for an individual, advantages once capitalised produce further advantages in competitive strength.

It will be seen, then, that choice of location, like any other business decision, is normally a rational decision, which is made after an assessment of the relative advantages of different locations for the purposes of the particular business. Moreover, it is one of the very early decisions in the foundation of an enterprise, and is all the more important in that it is one of the most difficult to reverse if the choice should prove to be unwise. In general it may be taken that the best location is that which will, other things being equal, facilitate the making of the greatest or most certain profit. No doubt there are some entrepreneurs who, through ignorance or for various non-business reasons, are content to receive lower returns, and to them a less suitable location may be acceptable. They are, however, a minority, and in any case in a competitive economy there is a pretty close limit to the disabilities that can be accepted or the positive advantages that can be foregone. Even in location decisions made by governments, where social cost calculations or strategic considerations may enter strongly into the reckoning, the purely economic side of proposals can seldom be completely ignored.

A final word on this part of the problem is concerned with changes through time. As new techniques are developed and new industries appear, so the circumstances in which location choices are made can change greatly, though the central problem of finding the location that gives the best combination of advantages remains the same. In Great Britain, for example, the development of efficient road transport both for people and for a wide range of industrial goods, the emergence in recent years of a whole congeries of new light industries, and the almost universal accessibility to energy supplies in the form of oil and of electricity from the national electricity grid, have made many industrial processes far more flexible in their location requirements than was true even as recently as the early inter-war years. This means that for many industries the crude attraction of nearby coal supplies or railway or port facilities has lessened; it does not mean that industrialists in these industries no longer have to consider the varying productive possibilities of different locations. Indeed, the greater the number of prima facie suitable locations the more refined becomes the choice and the greater the skill required to select the *best* location.* That this is recognised by industrialists is borne out by the reports of numerous local industrial development organisations that demands for very detailed information on their area are increasingly being made. Clearly, location decisions are being taken seriously and thorough preliminary investigation of possible areas is common, if not normal, procedure.

The actual nature of the location problem will of course vary with the kind and scale of operations in individual industries. The precise significance of location in the costs structure of some small firms and some 'light industries' may be a matter of controversy at the present time (unfortunately there is a dearth of adequate data and of objective studies of industrial costs in alternative locations[1]), but the number of industries for which location is a matter of indifference, or to which the terms 'mobile' or 'footloose' can be safely applied, is probably smaller than is commonly supposed. At the other end of the scale the location requirements of the large firm or basic industry are normally rigorous, and the correct location of such industries is a serious matter, not only for the firm itself but often also for the regional or even the national interest.

So far, we have not specified precisely what we mean by location. The word is commonly used in two different senses, a narrower one, in which it is equivalent to site, and a wider one, in which it indicates an area or a locality. The location influences with which we are concerned are essentially those that affect the

---

* It should be noted, however, that even the best location will probably not be wholly ideal: no location has a complete monopoly of advantages and complete absence of disadvantages, so that even the best choice will contain some element of compromise.

choice of an area or region. The choice of a site within an area is normally a second stage and demands local study, though it is true that sometimes exacting requirements of site may influence the choice of a region. Now regions, like countries, can vary greatly in size, and this fact introduces problems of scale and corresponding dangers. The United Kingdom, for example, has various well-recognized industrial areas, which differ in character and in which the variation of possible costs from one to another in any particular industry may be of importance. For some purposes, however, it may be more useful, as Professor M. J. Wise has emphasised to planners, to regard the whole country as a single industrial region. In some industries a manufacturer established in any recognised industrial area might not be badly placed to acquire his materials, to serve the greater part of the home market and to have adequate access to a port for overseas trade.

In the United States, on the other hand, with its vastly greater size, industrial areas are much bigger and far more widely separated. Location decisions, therefore, are often of a different order of magnitude and importance. New England, for instance, is recognised as a single industrial area in the United States, and has an area not far short of that of England, Wales and Scotland combined. It is true that area alone, especially where much of it is not used, is far from being the whole story, but when we remember that some other industrial areas in the United States are larger than the New England one and that a manufacturer may have to decide between New England and southern California, three thousand miles away, the general point will be readily agreed.

Although, then, even in a small country such as our own, the location decision could make all the difference in *some* industries between conspicuous success and moderate success or even failure, our arguments are more generally applicable to large areas with unified economies. It is mainly for this reason that many, indeed perhaps a majority, of our examples are chosen from the United States: the problems there are more analogous to those of a large part of the industrial world, in such countries as Canada, USSR, Australia, India or Brazil, for instance.

The argument up to this point has been directed to showing that location is an important aspect of industry, worth serious study by the industrial geographer. Now the geographer is concerned primarily with what exists on the ground *now*, and what now exists on the ground in the kind, amount, layout and functioning of industry is the result of innumerable *past* decisions on where to locate particular works. (Current decisions are naturally affecting future patterns.) It follows that satisfactory analysis of the present distribution of industrial activity can be made by the geographer only if he understands what guided the industrialist in making those decisions, and the plan of this book is to examine the points an industrialist has to consider in grappling with each of the three main categories of task he has to perform.

These tasks are, first, the purchase of his raw materials and the assembling of them at the point of production; secondly, the processing of these materials; and, thirdly, the distributing of his finished product to his market. Location will generally not affect either the price he has to pay for his raw materials from a given source or the price he gets for his finished product, but will obviously affect very directly the transfer costs he has to meet inwards for his raw materials and outwards for his finished product. It is perhaps not so immediately obvious that location, as location, can affect the costs of processing in his works, but it has in fact important effects that can make processing costs in one area different from those in another, though the effects vary considerably in importance from industry to industry. The industrialist, therefore, in arriving at his location decision has to balance these costs against one another in his endeavour to find the location that offers him the best, or most certain, returns.

In the following chapters we consider the various circumstances that influence transfer and processing costs. Not all of the forces influencing location, however, arise out of the nature and organisation of industry itself; some derive from outside influences, especially government activity, and such 'external' influences must be given due weight in our analysis. In practice the influences on location decisions are not independent but act and react on one another. For purposes of analysis and exposition, however, we must consider them separately, but, even where in our general treatment we give specific examples, it must be remembered that the particular influence being illustrated is only one of the many that are at work. We hope that our separate study of individual industries in Chapters 9 and 10 will illustrate better the real complexity of the location problem.

[1] Since the first edition of this book was published W. F. Luttrell has completed a 2-volume study of *Factory Location and Industrial Movement* which has thrown more light on the problem in the UK. But, while this work presents objective studies of the economics of a change of location by firms in several industries, such studies are still too scarce and, more important, adequate data are still not available for advanced research.

2

MATERIALS, MARKETS AND TRANSFER COSTS

IN INDUSTRIAL LOCATION

In this chapter we are concerned chiefly with *movement*, of material of all kinds from source to factory and of products from factory to market. In some industries the transfer costs incurred are so heavy that the chief location problem is to find the point where total transfer costs are lowest. These are the 'transport oriented' industries, well exemplified by iron and steel. Other industries are concerned with the costs and inconvenience of moving materials and products but will not need to give transfer costs the first place in their location decisions. In this chapter we shall attempt to assess some of the reasons why the costs and significance of movement vary so much from industry to industry.

The influence of materials

All manufacturing industry performs some operation, or a series of operations, upon a supply of materials, and all industrial establishments will therefore be concerned, although in widely varying degrees, with their location relative to their materials and to the costs of procuring them. Most material resources are not available to industry at equal cost irrespective of location, for they are generally distributed in a rather patchy manner over the earth, and costs of exploitation and distribution vary widely. Ores of metal, for example, so fundamental to many manufacturing processes, are not everywhere economically accessible, and manufacturing processes utilising them will be located (other things being equal) with regard to the costs of procurement. Similarly, reliable and adequate food surpluses above local need are to be found only in certain regions of the world, and industrial establishments processing foodstuffs will have problems of supply and procurement in the forefront of their location considerations. Industrial processes which draw upon the products of other manufacturers for their materials will also carefully weigh the advantages of a location close to their supplies against those of a location at some other point. In every case the regularity, reliability and costs of material procurement must be considered, although the power of such considerations to influence location decisions may vary according to a variety of circumstances apart from mere procurement costs.

A simple proposition may conveniently summarise the core of the problem of the role of materials supply in location decisions. The degree of attraction exercised by materials varies widely according to the materials themselves, the processes that use them and the techniques available in distribution and utilisation. At the outset it may be useful to remind ourselves of two simple fundamentals. First, not all manufacturing enterprises draw directly upon the products of extractive industries (mining, agriculture and forestry) for their essential supplies. Many utilise the products of another industry or process as their 'raw material', and the conditions of supply naturally differ greatly from those under which raw materials from the extractive industries are obtained. Secondly, industries rarely use only one material. More commonly they draw upon a number, for each of which the conditions of supply may differ, thus introducing a considerable complexity into the picture.

We may now proceed by examining the first portion of our proposition, i.e. that the extent to which the material has power to attract industry to itself will vary according to the material in question and the process using it. There are several straightforward cases here. Does the material in question, undergoing the process in question, lose a great deal of weight or bulk? Is the material a perishable one? What is its value per unit of weight? Is it possible for the process to use another material as a substitute for the one currently favoured? How many materials are used and in what proportions? The role of material procurement in location decisions will depend to a significant extent upon the answers to these questions, and each merits a brief discussion.[1]

Naturally, if the *material loses greatly in weight or bulk* in manufacture it will cause the industry to be attracted to the point of material production. In this way transport costs on useless waste matter are avoided. The greatest losses of weight and bulk are usually found in industries where the produce of extractive activity is utilised directly, and such industries tend to be strongly attracted to the raw material source. The manufacture of beet sugar is an excellent example, for the weight of the raw sugar extracted in a sugar-beet factory is only one-eighth of the weight of the materials (beet, coal and lime) used. Further, pulp and paper weigh about two-fifths of the pulp-wood used; butter, cheese and manufactured milk products weight only about one-sixth, in aggregate, of the weight of the materials used in the factory; while the weight of the pig iron produced from a blast furnace may be as little as one-third to a quarter of the materials charged.[2] Such processes are thus often found to be located in close proximity to their main raw materials. This simple proposition can be affected by other considerations, notably the structure of freight rate charges (which sometimes favours the transport of raw materials), by the possibility of a by-product arising out of the process, the disposal of which may affect the initial location decision, and by the economies to be gained by integration with other processes which have different location requirements.

The *degree of perishability of the material* is also of importance in assessing the strength of its attraction for manufacturing industry, for a perishable material, or one that travels badly, will naturally attract to itself the processes using it. Thus fruit and vegetable canning and preserving are often found near the sources of supply, and so are milk processing industries.

The *value of the raw material per ton* will also be significant, for a material of high value (e.g. wool) can more readily bear the costs of transport than a material of low value per unit of weight (e.g. copper ores). Transport costs will add less, proportionately, to the cost of a material of higher value than to one of lower value, and this despite the fact that railways and other forms of transport normally charge higher freight rates on more expensive than on less expensive commodities.

Further, the *possibility of using substitute materials* can strongly affect the decision whether or not to locate near the source of a given material. Among the considerations that will weigh in the choice of location for steel-making plant, for example, is the fact that either pig iron or scrap can form the main charge into the open-hearth furnace. Another possibility of substitution is in energy supplies, for many processes can meet their energy requirements from a variety of sources. This is examined separately in the following chapter. Here we should note that where materials are substitutable the pull of any *one* of them is reduced. This last point can be associated with the next.

The pull of the materials will depend on the *number of materials involved and their relative importance*. The attraction of one material in one direction may be countered by the pull of another in a different direction, and in general, as the number of materials used increases, the influence of any *one* will decline, unless it is one that loses much weight. The iron and steel industry, again, uses several important raw materials, and locations based on access to coal or to ore or to scrap can be found. Many modern industries, of which the radio and electrical product industries are good examples, use numerous materials. None of these materials is significantly weight-losing or perishable, and most of them are required in relatively small quantities. In such industries materials exert little, if any, influence on the location decision.

The influence of the materials as just discussed may, however, be reduced or enhanced by the *structure of freight rates*. This is examined in greater detail later, but the point may be usefully illustrated here by an example. Changing railway rate differentials as between livestock and meat products have been 'an important factor in the struggle between rival centres of the packing industry'[3] in the U S A. At first slaughtering and packing was favoured in the eastern states by a rate on livestock about one-third of the rate for beef. Chicago pressure subsequently brought the rate on the finished product down, enabling its packing industry to compete more effectively in the eastern market and therefore grow in size and importance. Following this the meat packing industry began to grow in centres yet farther west, and the Chicago packers then demanded lower rates on livestock to enable them to complete with these establishments which were even nearer the cattle ranges. Finally, percentage increases on all these rates has further favoured the movement of livestock and this stimulated the packing industry in the extreme east again.[4]

The connecting link between these various forces that increase or decrease the attraction of industry by materials lies therefore in the transport situation. It is the costs or difficulty of movement that prevent the free flow of materials to where they might ideally be required. From this it follows that material supply considerations tended to play a greater part in location decisions during times when transport facilities were not as highly developed as they are nowadays in advanced communities.

This introduces the second part of our initial proposition, which suggested that the influence of materials would vary according to the technological conditions of distribution and utilisation. Concurrently with advances in transport techniques, which will be dealt with later in the chapter, have come equally significant technical advances in processing which have decreased yet further the 'pull' of materials on a broad range of industries. One may cite the introduction of techniques of preliminary treatment of primary raw materials (e.g. beneficiation of iron and copper ores), reducing the quantity of waste and increasing their transportability. Again, by economies in manufacturing, the ratio of costs of materials at the works to total costs of production has been reduced.

For such reasons much industry is nowadays less seriously affected in its location, at least directly, by the location of its materials. From the examples given above, however, it is clear that material procurement costs do remain significant as a locating factor in some important industrial processes. Among these are certain industries engaged in the processing of the produce of extractive industries (i.e. processing 'raw material', in its literal sense, from farm, forest or mine), where most difficulties of bulk, waste content or perishability are still to be faced.

Thus saw-mills are normally located with strict regard for timber supplies and consequently, in the USA, the distribution of the industry shows marked shifts over time. This reflects the exhaustion of supplies in old-established areas (as in Michigan and Wisconsin) and the attraction of virgin forest resources elsewhere (as in the Pacific north-west). Copper smelting, too, is oriented towards its raw materials. Copper ore is very low in metal content (from about 0.5 to 7 per cent copper) and cannot readily bear the costs of transport. Although concentration of the ore at the mine decreases the waste element, smelting is most economically performed near the supply of ores, at a site where energy supplies are also available. The product of the smelter (blister copper) is relatively pure and can be transported long distances to the refineries, which therefore tend to be located near the market. Thus in USA most smelting capacity is in the west, where the ores occur, while about two-thirds of refining capacity is in the east, where copper-using industries are concentrated. When a sequence of operations is involved, then, a general tendency can be observed for the earlier processes in the manufacturing sequence, where primary raw materials are mainly used, to be attracted more strongly to the sources of their materials than are later processes in the sequence. This, let it be stressed, is an observable tendency and is by no means an invariable rule. It is true for the two examples given above and, as Smith has pointed out, for the iron and steel and steel product sequence, for the sugar-refining sequence and for others.

On the other hand there are important exceptions. Oil refining, for example, utilises a primary raw material directly, but the industry is not mainly found at the oil-producing location. The oil itself accounts for a high percentage of the total costs, a feature which, as we have seen, may often make a site near the producing area desirable. But in this case the loss of weight in processing is relatively small and the raw material is fluid and can be transported readily. Thus other factors become of greater importance; for example, the attractions of a location at a 'break of bulk' point (a port); of a location where oil supplies can be readily drawn from various oil-producing regions; or of a location near a market, where manufacturing and distributing economies can be gained. In all locations, however, consideration is given to convenience of access to supplies.

A final point needs to be made. Even where, on several counts, the pull of a material is strong, production may not be at or near the source of the material. Remoteness from markets, lack of labour, poor transport facilities or other such reasons (discussed later) may offset the pull of the raw materials and make utilisation at the point of origin uneconomic. Further, material-oriented industry may be located at a considerable distance from its materials, as when a country feels a need to possess such an industry but cannot provide all the essential resources. Such an enterprise is, however, best located at the point of minimum procurement cost, normally at or near a port when the material is being imported by sea, or at some nodal point if the material required is to be moved overland from its source to its destination. Thus considerations relating to material procurement will still play an important part in its location.

Market influences[5]

Despite the declining influence of raw materials on location decisions in most modern industry, it remains true that all entrepreneurs will be concerned to examine their situation with regard to their essential material supplies. But the attractions of a materials location often have to be measured against those of a location elsewhere, and notably of a market location. Before we proceed to examine these market influences it may be necessary to add that a 'market' is often more a derived than an original feature. A concentration of industry at any point creates a market at that point and a raw materials location can become a market location too. Similarly a market location can be a materials location for those who use the products of industry located there. In this context, however, we are chiefly concerned to discuss in isolation the function of market *as* market for location purposes, although its associated attractions must also be borne in mind.

The attractions of a market location have become of great significance for many modern industries. Among these industries are some in which the cost of moving the product to its market forms a high percentage of total costs. If the movement of the products to the consumer is more costly than movement of the materials to the factory, it may become desirable to locate as near as possible to the customer, who may be either the final consumer of the product or another industry. For such industries the attraction of the market, as market, like the attraction of materials, is made effective to a considerable extent through transfer costs. Again we find, therefore, that the 'pull' of the market can be affected by the prevailing structure of freight charges, and this point is considered below. In the meantime we may indicate several considerations that will influence a firm in deciding whether or not the most profitable location is one near the main market for its products. Several of these are naturally the converse of the forces attracting industry to its major materials.

First, an *increase in weight or bulk or fragility* in the product tends, other things being equal, to cause the producer to seek a location near his main market. In this class, for example, we find many of the industries that add water to their product. Each considerable city in America has its Coca-Cola bottling plant; breweries are often located in, or near, their main markets, though this can be modified by the 'selling power' of beer made with certain well-advertised waters and by the increasing use of cans instead of bottles. In the bakery processes there is also an increase of weight, bulk and perishability, for which reasons, among others, bakeries are strongly market-oriented. Further, the makers of rigid boxes, barrels and containers naturally seek a location near their main customers to avoid long-distance transport of their bulky products. In some cases even a process using bulky raw materials may find a location near its market more attractive. This can happen, for example, when the finished product is in small units, and economies can be obtained where long distances are involved by moving the raw material in large loads rather than the finished product in small packets. The household chemical industry in the United States is a good example.

A *high degree of perishability* in the product also makes a market location attractive, if not essential. Many foodstuffs are perishable, for example bread and cakes and ice cream. Makers of such products are preferably located close to the consumer. Other goods are perishable in a different sense and are closely tied to their major market. Local newspapers, for example, are of relatively little value outside their own localities, and newspaper production is thus strongly attracted to its market.

A market location is also desirable where *personal contact between producer and consumer* is necessary. Any industry which makes articles 'to measure' gains from proximity to its customers. This applies not only to the retail bespoke garment industry, but also to many manufacturing concerns which specialise in the production of small 'tailor-made' parts for other enterprises or for private customers. Most maintenance services need a market location. These can be considered as effectively part of the productive process, for without after-sales service many prospective purchasers will not buy. Some products may require an occasional service or overhaul at the factory and, in providing this, the factory gains from proximity to its customers. Thus, a 'large manufacturer of heavy electrical equipment which requires periodical factory reconditioning located a new plant in the Southwest (USA) in order to secure a larger share of the business in that area'.[6]

The production of a *relatively cheap commodity*, to whose selling price transfer costs can add substantially, also makes a location near a market attractive. This is true of cement manufacture, for example, where the high distribution costs of a heavy and low value product make access to the market a most important consideration in location.

The *size of the market area* is another consideration. 'To understand each plant location problem, the geographical market area which the plant intends to serve must first be clearly understood.'[7] The extent of the market may be local, regional, national or international and, in serving market areas of differing size, industries face very different locational problems. The size of the market area will be affected, among other things, by the nature of the market, which is therefore an associated consideration. If, for example, the market is a concentrated and specialised one, it would generally pay to be close to it. Thus, the manufacture of textile machinery is usually found in or near important textile centres. Similarly the farm machinery industry in the United States is located with access to the best market area in mind, i.e. largely in the Middle-West, while the new cotton-picking machines are being made chiefly in the south, where they will be used. This 'pull' of the main market region not only reflects the lower transfer costs on finished products, but also the advantages of personal contact between the makers and the users of the products, which 'gives impulses to inventions and improvements'.[8]

Conversely, if the market area is a widespread one, and the costs of distribution add appreciably to total costs, the industries serving it are commonly widespread also. Examples are again found in the baking, bottled beverages and ice industries and, of a different type, in building and furniture manufacture. Where, however, the output of relatively few enterprises serves a national or international market, the centre of production may be either near the main indigenous market (saving in transfer costs on the quantities sold therein) or at a good distribution point. The national market for electrical machinery in the USA, for example, is mainly served by an industrial concentration in the north-east. For firms with a large overseas market, a port possesses many attractions.

Market capacity can also affect the location decision. Some modern industries find maximum economies in production when they operate on a very large scale. The choice of location for such giant concerns will naturally be affected by the extent to which the 'local' market can absorb their output. The iron and steel industry is a case in point, and market capacity plays a considerable part in its location. Protracted consideration was recently given to the possibility of choosing a location in New England for a new integrated iron and steel mill. While New England was a desirable location in some respects, there was one overriding objection. The regional market could not absorb the full output of a modern plant, and to serve a wider market extra transport costs, which would be avoided by a coastal site farther south, would be incurred. Lack of market capacity is a grave handicap to the profitable development of such large modern industries as iron and steel, chemicals and automobile manufacture in non-industrialised or under-developed countries.

There are also, as has been intimated, other reasons for the attraction of industry to a market location. One is that a market is often a centre where materials occur not only for firms who wish to process further the products of other industries, but also for firms that use the waste products or scrap that arises. Shipbuilding centres and centres of automobile and machinery manufacture produce considerable quantities of steel scrap. This can be charged into open-hearth furnaces or electric steel furnaces, whose products find a market in the firms from which they obtain part of their material supplies. Other usable scrap and waste arise in a large market and attract processes that can utilise them.

Another advantage of a market centre with a large population is that it possesses a large and varied supply of labour, provides desirable services of many kinds and offers, in these and in other ways discussed later, possible economies in processing costs. A large centre is also an area of concentrated earning, and therefore spending, power. Such an area is thus very attractive to many enterprises producing final consumer goods, and is also a good location for new enterprises and for the development of new industrial processes.

For some enterprises the choice in location becomes a decision as between two or more possible market areas. An area where the outlook for the future is one of expansion of population and incomes might then prove highly attractive. A study of *Why Industry Moves South*[9] found that the major feature attracting industry to the southern states of USA in the post-war years was the increasing importance of these states as a market for industrial and consumer goods. Nevertheless an old and established area, as we shall see, may still possess advantages of its own.

Many students of the subject consider the attractions of the market to be so great that they regard a market location as now the 'norm' for modern industry. Locations other than market locations would then need to be explained by cost advantages that outweigh the attractions of the market and the cost of moving the product to its consumer. As we have seen, a raw material resource, among other things, may possess such advantages. The importance of a market location has, however, been much augmented by the general practice of charging higher freight rates on finished products than on raw materials, and we must now give more detailed attention to the effect of transport on location.

Transfer costs[10]

The importance of the part played by transport in industrial location has been implied in our study of materials and markets. Transport must be considered as an integral part of the productive process, for a commodity is useless until it has arrived at its point of consumption. The cost of assembling materials and distributing products varies in relative significance from one industry to another, but in some industries it forms a large proportion of total costs. Movement of goods over even quite short distances can seriously affect production costs. Thus, in a study of the Lorraine iron and steel industry, J. E. Martin[11] found that the high charges on the French railways for short hauls raised the ore costs for a works at a 'moderate distance' from a supplying mine by as much as 30 per cent. Such an increase in ore costs for even short-distance haulage is bound to affect the relative economies of production. Many industrial concerns, therefore, are acutely interested in the varying costs of transport in different areas and, other things being equal, would tend to locate where aggregate transfer costs are at a minimum. Even where the actual expenses incurred are not significant, however, the existence of an efficient transport *service* most certainly will be.

At the outset we should be aware that the costs of movement are not fully expressed by freight charges. Other costs that add materially to the total sum are also incurred, e.g. cost of insurance on goods and materials en route, interest charges on their capital cost, losses incurred by deterioration of or damage to the product in transit, clerical costs and so on. We shall, therefore, reserve 'transport costs' for direct freight costs of movement and use 'transfer costs' to include the indirect as well as the direct expenses. It behoves the producer to examine the type and quality of transport services available, for the speed, regularity and dependability of the services will be reflected in the 'indirect' costs of movement. Requirements vary, of course, with the nature of the commodity involved. For bulky and low value commodities speed is seldom a prime requirement. More important, as a general rule, is the ability of the transport medium to carry large quantities at a low price, and this affects the form of transport preferred. These commodities can be moved most cheaply by water, and the location of the establishments concerned may depend on the availability of adequate coastal, canal or river services. By contrast a highly perishable commodity requires, above all, speedy movement, and road, rail or even air transport services are preferred.

How transfer costs are made up

There are several important elements that affect the transfer costs incurred in any given location. The form of transport available, the distance to be covered and the type of terrain are obviously of importance. If different forms of transport are available, competition may cause special rates to be quoted. We may note as an example the effects of the New York State Barge Canal in the United States. Railway rates have had to take into account the existence of this alternative form of transport from the Lakes to New York. So freight rates from Chicago to New York have been lower than from Chicago to Philadelphia—even when freight was carried through Philadelphia on its way to New York.[12] It is interesting also to see that the opening of the St Lawrence Seaway in April 1959 brought an immediate reduction in railway rates on several commodities moving between Atlantic and Lakeside ports.[13]

The possibility of a return cargo has significance, for if wagons, barges and trucks have to return empty, freight charges must be high enough to pay the cost of their return journey. The nature of the commodity also affects the situation, extra costs being incurred if, for example, special containers are required (for liquids or for refrigerated goods), or special care (for fragile items), or special speed of movement (for perishable goods), or special loading and unloading facilities. Further, a large volume of traffic may induce transport agencies to offer special rates. This can have adverse effects on smaller firms in their competition with larger ones, and upon new enterprises, whose growth may be restricted by their having to absorb higher transfer costs than their larger competitors who qualify for freight rate reductions. It has been suggested[14] that this feature, in operation, would tend to stabilise existing industrial distributions, since new areas would find difficulty in establishing themselves.

The structure of freight rates is another element of extreme importance. 'Freight rates are to regions and to cities what tariffs are to nations.'[15] It is unfortunate, therefore, that the question of freight rates is exceedingly complex, and amenable only with great difficulty to geographical analysis, though techniques are being developed.[16] Gilbert Walker, for example, considered that there were probably about forty million different railway rates in the UK in the early 1940's, each rate being the price of a particular railway service.[17] Nationalisation has probably not altered this situation greatly. Since 1957 British Railways have been able to charge special undisclosed rates for any traffic they would like to encourage and it is likely, therefore, that the present situation is at least as complex as when Walker wrote. The situation for road transport is no simpler and there is no compulsion on operating companies, in the United Kingdom at any rate, to publish their rates. Road rates in fact vary from haulier to haulier for the same load, from customer to customer for the same haulier, from one kind of load to another and from one distance to another.

In spite of the general complexity of freight rate structure it is possible to make a few useful observations. Charges will, in the first place, vary according to the commodity to be carried. Bulky raw materials are often carried for less per ton-mile than semi-finished or finished products. The latter, being of higher value, can normally bear a higher transport charge, which will add less, proportionately, to the delivered cost. The relative rates for different products may affect location considerably. For example, if there is a sequence in the productive processes, as there is in the iron and steel industry, the location of each process in the series may depend on the existing structure of freight charges as it affects the various commodities to be moved.

'. . . if quantities of materials only are considered (weight of ore, coal and product), location would undoubtedly be pulled to ore or coal. But when comparative freight rates are considered the picture is very different. These cause the movement of the raw materials to be less costly than the subsequent movement of the steel to fabricating centres. The pull of the raw material is therefore reduced, and a market location becomes more profitable. Thus a significant quantity of new steel capacity in the USA is at the market.'[18]

In other words, the cheaper rates quoted for the heavy raw materials enable them to be transported further than would be economic if the same ton-mile rate were applied to raw materials and to finished products.

Freight rates also vary according to distance, as has been mentioned. But the structure of rates is generally such as to fall off per ton-mile with increasing distance, although not in uniform steps. A high proportion of the total costs of movement is incurred at terminals, i.e. they are costs of storage, loading and discharging. These are the same irrespective of length of haul, and the haulier can afford to quote less and less per ton-mile as the distance increases. In practice the rates move upwards in a series of steps, getting shallower and longer as distance increases. Sheer distance,

B

therefore, may be less of a handicap than one might at first think. Far more important is the necessity, where it occurs, to 'break bulk' and transfer the load to another form of conveyance. This raises costs sharply.

An 'artificial break' of bulk is often assumed at national boundaries, and loads crossing such boundaries, though they continue in the same conveyance, are often charged as if they were starting the journey anew. The economies of long-distance haulage are therefore lost, while other fictitious terminal charges are sometimes added. Such practices affect the movement of goods across national frontiers and the loss is felt on both sides. Thus an important task facing the European Coal-Steel Community on its establishment was to abolish such discriminatory practices in the movement of the relevant materials among the 'Six'. In this way all the members should eventually benefit from the greater con-centration of production in the most economic centres. To this end the High Authority imposed international through rates on the movement of fuel and ore in 1955–6 and of steel and scrap in 1956–7. This has had significant results in the freer flow of these commodities across the frontiers of the Community nations and is changing the boundaries of supply and market areas.

The operation of the freight-charging practices that have just been described can be modified and result in a type of location that must be explained with reference to the particular circum-stances. For example, 'fabrication in transit' privileges may permit the processing of a material to be carried on at a point along a transport route. This enables the producer, located between his material source and his markets, to obtain the 'savings' of a long haul, despite the fact that it is two relatively short hauls that have been made instead of one long one, and that the second part of the haul may comprise a very different commodity. Flour milling in the American prairies is an example: in some cases packed breakfast foods may emerge and continue the journey at the 'through-rate' for the grain. Similar arrangements are sometimes made for other commodities, including steel.[19] One reason for the granting of such privileges will be that the railways have an interest in establishing industries along their own lines, for this increases their traffic and makes competition for the trade less likely.

More important than in-transit privileges, however, is the operation of restrictive schemes imposed either by governments or by groups of producers acting in concert. The Pittsburgh Plus system (a basing point system) in the USA is a good example. This system, imposed by the major steel producers and in operation from 1900 to 1924, required that all steel be sold at the Pittsburgh price plus freight cost from Pittsburgh, no matter where it was produced or where it was sold. The effect was naturally to handicap the growth of the industry in new areas, and the existence of the scheme goes far to explain why such a large percentage of total iron and steel capacity in the USA remains in the Pittsburgh area. The system was replaced in 1924 by a multiple basing point scheme, but Pittsburgh was still strongly favoured in its operation. Other important centres increased their growth, but the system was nevertheless a real handicap to them. The 1924 scheme was abandoned in 1948, when it was declared illegal, and FOB pricing, in which the purchaser pays the actual costs of transport incurred, was established. Since then the importance of other areas of steel production has increased yet more rapidly.[20]

Just as the nature of transport facilities in early decades of the industrial age can be seen to affect the location of industrial activity today, so can the structure of freight rates in the past help to explain some present industrial concentrations. 'Pittsburgh Plus' was one example. A further important example in the USA was the existence of five official freight-rate territories up to 1952. Within each of these territories a broadly similar structure of freight rates applied, but between them large differences occurred. These inter-regional differences strongly favoured the north-eastern states. They 'gave the Northeast a definite rate advantage making it less expensive, on the average, to ship goods in that region than in any other part of the nation. . . . [The] effect of the regional differences in class rates which prevailed from 1887 to 1952 will be observable in the regionalisation of the American economy for many years to come.'[21]

Such special circumstances apart, normal transfer costs have played, and do play, an important part in location decisions in industry and affect the competitive position of individual producing areas. These 'normal' transfer costs are related to the distances and the kinds of terrain over which transport has to be done. New England, for instance, is located in the extreme north-eastern corner of the United States and is separated from the interior by the difficult mountain country of its western border. Only by sea can raw materials come in and finished products go out cheaply and, so long as its sources of supply lay in the West Indies and the Atlantic coast of America and its chief markets in Europe, New

England had a position supremely good in America for the development of an industrial region. When, however, the United States turned its face westwards and population and markets grew in the interior, where, as it happened, there was enormous wealth of coal, iron ore and other raw materials, the peripheral position of New England placed it industrially at a distinct disadvantage against the competition of the newer industrial regions farther west. That this is still the case was brought out very clearly in a post-war survey of industry in New England by the Federal Reserve Bank of Boston: one-third of the respondents stated that they were operating under a severe handicap in transfer costs. This fact alone goes far towards explaining the present industrial character of New England, with its absence of heavy industry and its concentration on a variety of metal manufactures (mechanical and electrical machinery and electronic products, for example) of high quality and high value per unit of weight.

To revert to the considerations affecting individual enterprises, for the 'transport-oriented' industries the best location is one that minimises the costs of procurement and distribution. Sometimes the issue may be relatively straightforward. Thus, other things being equal, wherever the product is much lighter or less bulky than the materials used, the process is likely to be attracted towards the material source. As we have seen, copper smelting is an example. Alternatively, if the product is more expensive to transport than the materials, as in cement manufacture, production is more likely to be at or near the market.

In other cases, however, although transfer costs remain significant, a compromise will be required, as, for example, where several materials are used and none of them is predominant or where a wide market is to be served. A location may then be chosen because of its accessibility from or access to a wide area. An example of a modern industry of this kind, mainly concerned with the assembly of parts drawn from a wide area, is the British motor vehicle industry. Its perceptible concentration in the English Midlands illustrates the desirability of a nodal position for the collection at the assembly plants of the component parts, and for the distribution of the finished product to the home market. In the USA the manufacture of finished automobiles is strongly concentrated in an area centred on Detroit—an area well placed to serve the very large market of the north-east industrial belt. But the production here of car engines and component parts is even more strongly concentrated than the final assembly of the vehicle, which is being increasingly performed at locations selected for access to market areas elsewhere in the country. The reason is that the transfer costs on a 'knocked-down' vehicle are but a fraction of those on the made-up product.

Finally we should remind ourselves that a location where total transfer costs are at their lowest is not necessarily the location most favourable for an industrial enterprise. There remains a broad group of other important influences in which transfer costs do not play a part. A location which provides low processing costs may often be preferred to the one providing low assembly and distribution costs. The decision will depend on whether the additional transfer costs are compensated by the savings in processing costs. We shall turn to the factors making for low processing costs in a later chapter. First, however, a glance at the historical development of transport facilities may afford a useful illustration of the actual effects of transport systems upon the location of industry in modern times.

The historical importance of transport

Little advance can be made towards functional and areal special-isation on a commercial scale until an efficient transport system is developed. The beneficial results of the agrarian and indus-trial revolutions, therefore, could be obtained only by develop-ment of new methods of bulk movement and by capital invest-ment in transport lines and equipment. In the early stages of the industrial age the difficulty of transport acted very strongly upon the location of industrial enterprise. At first all inland transport was slow and highly expensive. Consequently, coastal towns, estuarine towns and towns on navigable rivers were favoured for commercial activities, Antwerp, London, Bristol and Bruges being good examples.

Canal construction was stimulated by, and in turn stimulated, the early progress of the industrial revolution in Britain, and was preceded and accompanied by schemes of river improvement.[22] Without the improved water transport facilities little development of large-scale industry would have been possible in Britain at that time. Naturally the expensive artificial routeways were mainly oriented towards the essential bulky raw materials, above all to coal, and they attracted industrial processes to their banks. The limitations of the canals, however, were severe, and as the industrial age progressed and the railways appeared these defects became more apparent, more undesirable and less necessary to endure. Canal traffic was slow, moving at a walking pace and interrupted by numerous locks; the canals were narrow and could take barges of only shallow draft; there was difficulty in maintaining adequate depth of water in dry seasons, while freezing hampered their utilisation in winter. Improvements were made difficult by the buildings along the banks and, when competition from the railways was intensified in the second half of the nineteenth century, capital investment was discouraged by the falling traffic. Some railway companies purchased canals and allowed them to fall into disuse. Such circumstances account for the decline in canal traffic in the United Kingdom, but it would be difficult to overstress their early contribution to industrial activity.

Elsewhere, water-borne traffic has also been of immense importance in influencing the patterns of industrial distribution. As Pounds comments on the Ruhr:

'the development of the Ruhr into one of the foremost industrial areas of the world has been made possible only by the development of the means of transportation. . . . Transport costs are a relatively high proportion of total costs and the situation would be a great deal more adverse if intensive use were not made of water transport. . . . Although the rivers and canals carry only a small fraction of the total freight transported within the Ruhr . . . [they have] exceptional importance.'[23]

In the United States the Erie Canal accelerated immensely the rise of New York and the development of the Middle West. With the opening of the canal in 1825 the Buffalo–New York journey was reduced from twenty days to eight and the freight rate from $100 to $5 a ton.[24] Industrial activity was promoted not only at both ends of the canal but also in the cities that developed along its length. With the advent of the railways its relative decline was inevitable, but, enlarged and improved, and re-christened the New York State Barge Canal, it still carries a not inconsiderable amount of traffic and by its very existence acts as a check upon the raising of railway rates along its route.

The railways permitted far greater flexibility in the movement of goods and raw materials, were speedier, and easier to construct and maintain. They allowed a readier movement of raw materials to a greater variety of locations and thus aided industrial growth at centres away from the coalfields. The initial result in the United Kingdom, however, was to emphasise the pattern of major industrial location on the coalfields. Industry was still using great quantities of coal at comparatively low efficiencies and many materials could be readily brought to the coalfield, while the products could be efficiently distributed by rail. The coalfields, often with associated iron-ore supplies, had attracted the major industries in the canal era and they consequently continued to offer many attractions to industry even after the development of a substantial railway network. On the Continent, however, where the main development of large-scale factory industry followed the construction of the early railways, industry tended from the start to be rather more widespread in its location than in Britain, although the coalfields still attracted major concentrations. In general, access to rail transport became so highly desirable that many firms possessed their own private sidings. Although the 'pull' of rail transport has greatly diminished in recent decades, the proximity of good rail connections still remains an important location consideration for a wide range of manufacturing processes.

The twentieth century has brought road transport to the fore. Many modern industries find the unparalleled flexibility of the automobile of great value both in the procurement of their materials and in the distribution of their products. Most modern light industries, and some heavy industries, find that road transport competes successfully with rail even over long distances. In the United Kingdom, Ministry of Transport estimates suggest that goods vehicles carried about 56 per cent of total ton-miles of traffic in 1958, an increase in volume of about 25 per cent since 1952. In the United States, too, although distances to be covered are much greater and therefore more favourable to movement by other forms, road transport has been gaining ground steadily (see Table 1, p. 40). Coast-to-coast movement of goods by truck is quite common, and even bulky goods and raw materials are carried.

The close timing of deliveries of materials by road brings substantial economies. When delivery is erratic, or involves large quantities in a single delivery, capital is tied up in stocks and in storage space and equipment. Efficient use of road transport enables delivery to be more closely co-ordinated with production and the manufacturer can treat the highway as virtually part of his conveyor-belt system. At the other end of the process distribution by road can similarly provide substantial economies.

The modern manufacturer must also consider the growing tendency for his employees to come to work by private vehicle. To some extent this may absolve him from ensuring that his new factory is easily accessible by existing public transport but it also involves him in greater land requirements for parking. This may be considered a little remote from the real considerations that affect the industrialist in his choice of site, but it is, in fact, of growing importance. A recent study of industrial problems in central Detroit[25] found that, where firms wished to leave their existing sites and quoted the need for extra room as their main reason, the need for parking space was cited more often than the need for additional productive floor space.

TABLE 1

VOLUME OF DOMESTIC INTER-CITY FREIGHT TRAFFIC
BY TYPE OF TRANSPORT, USA
Selected years

Year	Total volume in billions* of ton-miles	Rail- ways	Motor vehicles	Inland water- ways†	Oil pipeline	Airways
		%	%	%	%	%
1940	0·65	63·2	9·5	18·1	9·1	0·002
1950	1·09	57·4	15·8	14·9	11·8	0·029
1960	1·34	44·3	22·2	16·4	17·0	0·057
1962	1·41	43·7	23·6	15·8	16·9	0·083

Source: Statistical Abstract of the United States, 1964, table 787
*A ton-mile is the movement of a ton (2,000 lb) of freight for one mile. A billion = one thousand million in USA
†Including Great Lakes

For valid reasons, then, new roads near major centres of population prove an irresistible magnet to industry. The possibilities of using road transport on a large scale are sometimes said to have had an 'explosive' effect on industrial location, permitting factors other than proximity to rail or water transport to play a greater part in location decisions for an ever widening range of industries. 'Divorced from water and even rail transport [many new factories] have wedded themselves to rubber tyres for moving both freight and workers.'[26]

Other forms of transport are possible and can influence location decisions. We may mention, for example, pipelines, which are already important carriers of fluids or gases, and may become important for the movement of pulverised materials, e.g. coal. Piped supplies of natural gas have encouraged the location of new developments in the glass industry of USA closer to the main markets in the north-east. Aircraft, too, are growing in importance for moving special cargoes, and their use will certainly extend. So far they have had little influence on the location patterns of industry in general, but developments such as that at Shannon, Ireland,[27] may have more than a local interest and significance.

All forms of transport available and suitable at the present time ought to be considered in determining the best location for any new enterprise in which transfer costs are significant. But the transport conditions of the past are of great importance in understanding the present location of many major industrial areas. As we shall see later, established centres of production have great advantages to offer industrialists, even though the reasons for their original attraction of industry may have disappeared. For many such centres the *raison d'être* is to be found in the transport conditions of a century or more ago and, as always in the interpretation of the existing economic landscapes, we must delve a little into the past to achieve real understanding of the present.

[1] Location by materials had been closely studied by Wilfred Smith before his untimely death in 1955, and we shall use some of the results of his work. Among his publications, two are particularly useful in this context: 'Geography and the Location of Industry' (Inaugural Lecture), 1951; 'The Location of Industry' (Presidential Address), *Transactions of the Institute of British Geographers*, 1955. Many useful examples and studies may be found in his *An Economic Geography of Great Britain*, 2nd ed., 1952

[2] W. Smith, *Transactions of the Institute of British Geographers*, 1955

[3] D. P. Locklin, *Economics of Transportation*, 1938, p. 120

[4] See Locklin, op. cit.

[5] For a detailed study see C. D. Harris, 'The Market as a factor in the localisation of industry in the United States', *Annals of the Association of American Geographers*, 1954

[6] G. E. McLaughlin and S. Robock, *Why Industry Moves South*, 1949, p. 24. This book contains many excellent examples and uses actual case histories

[7] Ibid, p. 32

[8] G. Alexandersson, *The Industrial Structure of American Cities*, 1956, p. 45

[9] McLaughlin and Robock, op. cit.

[10] Transfer costs are studied in some detail by E. M. Hoover in *The Location of Economic Activity*, 1948

[11] 'Location Factors in the Lorraine Iron and Steel Industry', *Transactions of the Institute of British Geographers*, No. 23, 1957

[12] J. R. Smith and M. O. Phillips, *North America*, 1942, p. 167

[13] *The Times Review of Industry*, May 1959

[14] James and Jones (Eds.), *American Geography, Inventory & Prospect*, 1954, p. 325.

[15] H. E. Moore, quoted in J. W. Alexander, S. E. Brown and R. E. Dahlberg, 'Freight Rates: Selected Aspects of Uniform and Nodal Regions', *Economic Geography*, January 1958

[16] See J. W. Alexander and others, op. cit.

[17] G. Walker, *Road and Rail*, 1942

[18] A. Rodgers, 'Industrial Inertia, a major factor in the Location of the Steel Industry in the United States', *Geographical Review*, 1952

[19] See Locklin, op. cit., p. 125 f.

[20] For a detailed study of the operation and effects of 'Pittsburgh Plus' see G. W. Stocking, *Basing Point Pricing and Regional Development*, 1954

[21] J. W. Alexander and others, op. cit., p. 4

[22] Navigable conditions on an important waterway are discussed by W. G. East in 'The Severn Waterway in the Eighteenth and Nineteenth Centuries', chapter VI, *London Essays in Geography* (ed. Stamp and Wooldridge), 1951

[23] N. J. G. Pounds, *The Ruhr*, 1952, pp. 203–4

[24] Smith and Phillips, op. cit., p. 89

[25] H. Black, 'Detroit. A Case Study in the Industrial Problems of a Central City', *Land Economics Quarterly*, August 1958

[26] Federal Reserve Bank of Boston, *Annual Report*, 1955

[27] The Shannon Free Airport Industrial Estate was set up with the intention of using air freight almost exclusively in manufacturing and associated operations. It lies in a Free Trade Zone where materials, equipment and products can enter or leave without duties or customs formalities. Established manufacturing enterprises include electronic components, precision fasteners, transistor radios, clothing—i.e. products normally having a high value to weight ratio, as would be expected in these circumstances. (These developments have, however, been supported by government financial and other incentives.)

3

ENERGY SOURCES AND INDUSTRIAL LOCATION

The energy requirements of manufacturing processes can be met from various sources. Animals and man himself can provide a limited motive force; vegetable sources, especially timber, can be used to provide heat; water power, used directly, and winds are other means of obtaining motion; while coal, oil and natural gas may be used to generate heat, which in turn can provide a motive force. We may divide these sources of energy into 'capital' and 'income' sources. The world's main capital reserves are coal and lignite, peat, oil from oil shales, petroleum and natural gas. Income energy is derived from the continuing activity of the sun, which sustains vegetative growth, animal life and the constant movement of air and water, all of which may be harnessed for use in industrial processes at varying scales.

The significance of the division lies in the fact that the capital sources are irreplaceable whereas income sources are continuously renewed. By far the greater proportion of energy used in manufacturing is derived from the irreplaceable resources of coal, petroleum and natural gas. Little significant industrial activity is based on the renewable sources, with a few notable exceptions, although the earth receives as income from the sun an energy equivalent of about seventeen million millions of tons of coal per annum.[1] In the present state of technology, however, only an infinitesimal fraction of this energy can be harnessed by man. A. Parker estimates the coal equivalent of available energy from wood, waterpower and winds to be about 4·2 thousand million tons per annum, only about one-fifth of which could be harnessed

at present.[2] Even though it may prove possible to harness these
quantities of income energy, a rapid growth in their contribution
to industry's needs is unlikely. By contrast the capital energy
resources are given by Parker as being equivalent to only about
six million millions of tons of coal, of which, however, about half
could be harnessed economically.

Such theoretical reserves are hardly significant to us in our
present task. We have to consider the importance of actual and
immediately possible energy supplies to industry and their effects
upon its location, and to this end we shall confine ourselves to the
major fuel and power sources for modern industry, i.e. coals,
petroleum, natural gas and, far behind all these, water power. It
should be remembered that these energy sources can be utilised
either directly or indirectly by industry. In other words, modern
industry often has a choice both of the type of primary energy
source to use and of the form in which to use it. Direct use implies
a location either on the site of exploitation or at a point to which
the energy source can be brought economically. Used indirectly,
the primary energy source is converted to energy in another form,
which may be either more convenient or cheap to use or to
transport. Thus coal and oil may be used to produce gases for
industrial use—as a fuel or power source in this context and not
as a raw material. Although the industrial use of such gases has
increased, however, their supply has not had an important
locating influence. More important for location decisions is the
fact that any primary source can be used to generate electricity.
Cost considerations will, in the absence of political and other outside influences, decide from which source electricity is generated.

The *demand* for, and form of, energy used by any given industry
will, other things being equal, vary according to the requirements
of the processes involved and the cost of procuring supplies.
Energy is demanded in different forms by different industries. In
some the main demand is for heat, as in smelting, in some food
processes and in some industrial heat treatments. In others it is
needed mainly to provide a motive force to drive machinery or to
move materials and products. In yet others it is required for
chemical and electrolytic processes. In meeting its energy requirements an industry may be able to choose among various possible
sources. A heat treatment, for example, can often use any primary
source. Which one is used will depend on conditions and costs of
supply and on various technical and other considerations in the
establishment concerned. A motive force can be provided using

steam from coal firing or steam from oil firing, or from internal-combustion engines or electric motors. To a certain extent, therefore, we may regard the various sources of energy as being *possible* substitutes for one another in a wide range of industrial uses, but not in all. In certain processes substitution may be impossible, or, if feasible, uneconomic in the present state of technology. Among the most important of such processes is the use of coke in blast furnaces, for which no economic substitute is yet possible, and blast furnace location is consequently still strongly affected by coking coal requirements. (Note, however, that coke in the blast furnace is a raw material as well as a fuel.)

The possibility of substituting one source of energy for another in many industries, however, has been important in bringing about changing emphases in the location of industry over time. It is clear that technological advance has progressively altered the conditions of demand for energy, permitting the growth of new industries (e.g. those requiring enormous quantities of heat) and the substitution of one energy source for another where economies were to be gained by such substitution. In consequence corresponding changes have been made in the patterns of industrial location.

On the *supply* side we must note important variations in availability of energy over space and time. Variations in the quality, accessibility and general costs of exploitation of known resources, as well as the unequal distribution of energy resources over the world, cause great inequalities between areas in the costs of energy. The USSR, for example, possesses about one-half of estimated world coal and lignite reserves while the Australasian share amounts to less than 1 per cent. The Middle East dominates the picture of known world oil reserves, having more than one-half of the currently proven total. One-third of estimated world water power potential is in Latin America. That the mere existence of resources is only part of the story, however, is amply illustrated in the last example, the vast energy potential of Latin America being as yet scarcely touched. With such regional inequalities in energy resource the economics (and politics) of the transport of energy assume great significance. The transportability of its energy plays a major part in deciding whether or not a known resource can be exploited, and which of several possible sources of energy will actually be used in any given location. It is clear, then, that energy supply and costs can vary widely as between industrial regions.

The time variations in supply, as in demand, are related to technological advances that made previously unused or little-used sources of energy available to manufacturing industry, or enabled one source of energy to be substituted for another. Such advances have also had important repercussions upon the location of industrial activity, as will be shown below.

The main uses of energy, as indicated above, are to generate heat and to provide a motive force. It is useful to distinguish between fuel requirements (for heat) and power requirements (for motion), for this distinction can be of much significance in the industrial structure of regions where fossil fuels are relatively scarce and water power is relatively abundant. While the fossil fuels can be used economically both to provide industrial heat and also to supply motion by a variety of methods, water power is at the present time used significantly only in the production of electricity which, while a convenient and economic source of motive power, cannot be generally used as an economic source of heat. Electricity is an economic source of heat in the electro-metallurgical and electro-chemical processes, which require enormous quantities of energy that are often readily and relatively cheaply obtained at a site close by a hydro-electricity station. Conversely, in those processes where only very small quantities of heat are required, electricity can also be used to advantage. But for a wide range of other processes requiring heat (and heat is necessary at some stage in almost every modern industry) electricity cannot usually compete in cost with the more direct use of fossil fuels. Thus while fossil fuels in a region can provide an adequate energy base for almost the whole range of modern industry, water power as the predominant energy source will provide a satisfactory basis for only a selected group (and, even in this limited group, is subject to increasing competition from modern thermal power stations). Such considerations have had great influence on the industrial structure of central Canada[3] and the Pacific north-west of the United States of America.[4]

In analysing the effects of energy supply on industrial location, we may usefully adopt a chronological approach.

Early sources of energy for industry

Before the second half of the eighteenth century the most potent restriction on the location of any considerable industrial activity was the need for a food surplus above the requirements of the local agrarian population. But within the areas where there was food for industrial workers the need for fuel and for power in certain industries in quantities beyond that provided by human or animal muscle caused the main locations to be where fuel (mainly wood) and power from water and wind were available. This was true, for example, of flour mills, fulling mills, iron making and metal working, grinding and polishing.

The direct use of water power was a very important stage in industrial development, and the quantity of power provided reached significant proportions, judged by the standards of the times. There were, however, technical and economic limitations to its use. Techniques of harnessing and applying the power were not adequate to exploit the larger flows, while capital requirements were large relative to the quantity of power obtained. By the time these difficulties could be overcome, coal was forming an alternative source of power in western Europe, and water power sites became of decreasing importance in the location of industry, although small-scale operations continued for many years. The famous eighteenth-century Wortley wrought-iron works near Sheffield, for example, with its two water-driven tilt hammers and its blower, continued in operation until 1929. Survivals still remain in the textile industry, as in Perthshire,[5] while the location of many existing textile mills dates from the time when they were powered by water, although they have long since changed to coal or oil.

The direct use of water power continued to be important in industrial location along the Altantic coast areas of north-east USA for some time after it had begun to decline in the United Kingdom, and steam power played little part in manufacturing until the mid-nineteenth century. Here, in north-east USA, significant advances were made in the direct use of water power. The technical problems of harnessing larger, and therefore more reliable, flows and of building larger dams to control the water were being overcome. Greater volumes of power available at a single location permitted the concentration of industry in manufacturing towns (e.g. Lowell, Lawrence, Patterson) as opposed to the dispersed locations that resulted when establishments harnessed their own small sources. Improvements in water wheels increased efficiency and in the 1830's the turbine wheel was perfected. Although its most important application was to come much later, the turbine wheel began to replace the old bucket-type water wheel in the 1840's, thus enabling existing water power resources to be used more effectively. This served, however, but to postpone slightly the inevitable change from water power to steam, a change which brought here, as in Europe, profound consequences for industrial location.

The direct use of water power must not be dismissed, though, as of no account in the interpretation of present-day industrial distributions. In some areas the developments based, among other things, on water power were on such a scale and established such traditions and skills that a continuance of industrial activity was assured—as in Siegerland, Lancashire, the West Riding of Yorkshire and north-eastern USA.

New ideas and new locations

The new ideas referred to here relate to developments in the industrial use of energy from coal, which have their main roots in the eighteenth century. Coal was used by industry in earlier times —in lime burning, brewing, glass making and dyeing, for example —but its use was barely tolerated in towns before the seventeenth century. Serious shortages of wood began to make coal a respectable fuel in the seventeenth century, but in the eighteenth new discoveries and inventions promoted a wider use of coal both as a fuel and as a source of power.

Latent in the Newcomen steam engine and also in the use of coke in iron smelting by Darby early in the eighteenth century were not only the revolution in industrial techniques but also a revolution in industrial location. The first impact was felt in the United Kingdom towards the end of the eighteenth century and during the following century elsewhere. The use of coke in smelting was not widely known until the latter part of the eighteenth century, but the method then spread gradually and attracted the iron smelting industry to the source of coking coal—normally in the first instance to where this fuel was associated with Coal Measure iron ores. Further developments in the iron industry also used coal as a fuel (e.g. Cort's puddling process, 1784) and re-emphasised the attractions of coalfields. Meanwhile Watt greatly increased the efficiency of the steam engine (c. 1769) and a short time later discovered how to convert the vertical motion into a rotary motion. Such advances enabled steam power to be used as a prime mover for industrial machinery and in locations away from the pit-head. Subsequent developments by George Stephenson and others enabled steam power to be applied to transport.

Such new ideas again led to new locations. Steam overcame the serious limitations of water, being more reliable and, within limits, more mobile. Because of the inefficiency, by modern standards, of the steam engine at this time, and because of transport limitations, the optimum location for many industries was where large quantities of coal could be procured economically—on the coalfield. This was the principal reason for the growth of the great industrial concentrations on the coalfields of the United Kingdom beginning in the last decades of the eighteenth century and continuing throughout the nineteenth century.

Elsewhere these developments came rather later, but no less inevitably. In the United States, for instance, as late as the 1830's the location of industry was still chiefly determined by water power and coal was a supplementary source. Coal was important in certain processes requiring heat (e.g. in iron works and glass manufacture) and, since coal was already being used as a fuel, such industries often used it as a motive force also. But steam power was not important in the overall picture. In Rhode Island, for example, 128 textile mills used water power and only four used steam as late as 1834. Even in Pennsylvania, where coal was more easily available and water power resources were not so good, only 57 out of 161 plants used steam for power in that year. Steam power was apparently more expensive than water even where coal was available locally. In 1839 the annual cost per horse power generated at Easton, Pennsylvania, a point quite close to anthracite, was $23 for water power and $105 for steam.[6] Nevertheless, steam power was thought to possess certain advantages. In textile manufacture, for example, it gave a more uniform speed and enabled finer-grade materials to be produced; while the greater freedom of location permitted by using coal encouraged some enterprises to adopt steam power and locate at points of advantage, such as the larger cities.

By 1850 the use of steam was growing, even in the important textile industries of New England, where water power was the only locally available energy source and the coal had to be 'imported'. Large factories using steam power were built at Portsmouth, Salem, Providence, Fall River and New Bedford, for example, for a variety of reasons. One was that existing water power resources were being severely taxed. The alternative was to use coal, and new locations utilising steam power were chosen with reference to accessibility to seaborne coal supplies. These locations, at the coast, also facilitated the procuring of raw materials and the distributing of the product. Moreover, capital from extensive shipping interests was available at these locations and, following the discovery (1859) and development of the

Pennsylvanian oilfield, the capital originally invested in the whale-oil industry was also seeking new outlets and became important in the growth of the textile industry of New Bedford.

The introduction of the water turbine was, as we have seen, only a short-term palliative to the inadequacies of direct water power, and improving transport conditions lowered coal costs and broadened the area of application of coal energy in USA. The situation in the last decades of the nineteenth century was one in which industrial activity in general was expanding, calling for larger and larger quantities of fuel and power; in which the costs of utilising water power direct were rising and the costs of coal energy were generally declining. Between 1870 and 1880 steam surpassed water as a power source both in the number of units operating and in the total power produced,[7] and coal was an important factor in location decisions. But, since coal was increasingly mobile and was being used with increasing efficiency, it became more and more possible to study other cost advantages of prospective locations, and energy supplies became but one of a number of considerations.

Technical advances, especially towards the end of the nineteenth century, tended therefore to decrease the pull of coal on industry. But major coalfields had by this time other advantages to offer industry—fixed capital investment, labour supplies, communication networks and markets, for instance—and thus continued to attract industry. Important economies continued to be obtained in the use of coal both as a fuel (e.g. in the metal-working industries) and as a power source in the steam engine. In the latter, for example, high-pressure boilers, progressively more compact and more economical in their fuel requirements, were developed, while improvements in construction, in water use and in lubrication enabled them to run for longer periods without being taken out of service. The turbine principle was also adapted to steam in the 1880's, and proved especially important in electricity generation.

Coal requirements per horse power generated had thus fallen greatly since the early inventions. Newcomen's first steam engine has been estimated to need about 20 lb of coal per horse power hour, which Smeaton later reduced to about 16 lb. Watt's engine consumed about 6–8 lb per horse power hour. In 1900 some 5 lb per horse power hour was common, and in 1924 about 1 lb in electricity generation using large turbines.[8]

Thus many of the new ideas on which the industrial revolution was built were concerned in some way with the introduction of, or greater use of, coal as a source of energy, replacing vegetable fuels and water power, and such developments had far-reaching repercussions on the location of manufacturing activity. Coal still provides a large proportion of world industrial energy requirements, but faces increasing competition. Statistics of energy consumption by source are given and discussed below, but before we turn to examine the merits of coal's competitors it is pertinent to note that coal still has many advantages as an industrial energy source, quite apart from its value as a raw material, and the older coalfield locations still have considerable importance. We may recall that there is still no economic substitute for coking coal in iron smelting and, since coal costs are an important element in total costs for this industry, the availability of coal remains an important consideration in location. For many other industries already located on the coalfields coal is still the cheapest energy source. Much capital is invested in coal burning equipment and, where establishments are already organised on a basis of coal energy, coal has a good head start over its competitors—but can maintain its position only so long as conditions of supply and price do not force it out of the market. Further, coal remains abundant, although costs of extraction tend to increase steadily over time, and is often found in countries where there are no important known reserves of oil or natural gas. In such countries the use of coal may be considered politically and economically desirable, as it saves foreign exchange and keeps indigenous mining capacity in good shape for emergencies. Domestic coal supplies can be reasonably assured while the supply and price of imported sources of energy can be subjected to external economic or political pressure. The industrial use of coal remains, therefore, of great importance and still plays a part in location decisions, although it is of much less significance than in the nineteenth century.

New primary sources

Just over a century ago (in 1859) the first oilwell was sunk in western Pennsylvania and kerosene began to replace whale oil as a source of light. Subsequently, as the techniques of using oil were developed (mainly in the present century), this new energy source opened up new industrial possibilities and began also to compete with coal in established transport and industrial uses, encouraging repercussions on industrial location. Although coal and oil are in many ways complementary fuels in a balanced industrial economy, oil has often made headway at the expense of coal. This should not be interpreted as suggesting that coal is, and was, an unsatisfactory energy source utilised in the absence of something better. Coal remains of high value and an essential fuel in many industries, but during the period of its near monopoly it invaded many markets for which it is no longer ideally suitable. Transport is a good example. Oil fuels overcome many of the disadvantages of coal, and it may be useful to describe their comparative merits briefly at this point.

The outstanding advantage possessed by oil is its transportability. Being a liquid it is relatively easily handled in loading and discharging while, unlike coal, it is not damaged in transit. A ton of oil occupies less volume than an average ton of coal and, more important, has a higher energy value. An average ton of bituminous coal contains roughly twenty-seven million British Thermal Units, while an average ton of crude oil contains approximately forty-five millions. Such considerations cause the ton-mile cost of moving energy in the form of oil to be lower than that for coal, an important advantage of oil. Further, although in its first cost to industry, in coal economies such as our own, oil is normally dearer per ton than coal, this is offset both by its higher calorific value and by the special properties and other advantages it offers in transport and certain industrial uses. Oil fuel is clean and relatively convenient in use; it is a more easily controllable fuel in combustion; it leaves no ash and is relatively easily stored, handled and moved once the necessary equipment has been installed. Its great mobility makes it an ideal power source for transport, and oil-derived fuels are being increasingly adopted in transport uses at the expense of coal. Oil is also increasingly biting into the industrial market for static uses of energy, even in regions where coal is abundant. Refineries in the UK increased their output of fuel oils by some 75 per cent between 1958 and 1962, chiefly in response to the rising demand from many industries. In steel manufacture, for example, the use of oil in open hearth furnaces has been growing rapidly, allowing closer control of the steel-making process and shortening the process time, while permitting certain furnace modifications which have raised furnace capacities, occasionally by as much as 25 per cent.[9] In other industrial uses oil is permitting considerable economies.

'Reheating furnaces converted to oil can handle up to 30 per cent more material with less furnace maintenance and a reduced labour requirement. . . . In the heavy clay industry productivity has been raised by as much as 40 per cent as a result of firing kilns with oil . . . [and] . . . where cleanliness is of prime importance, as in bakeries and food factories, oil is a much favoured fuel.'[10]

Much of what has been said about oil applies also to natural gas, the industrial uses of which have also been growing. It is again a fuel of high calorific value, clean and easy to use. Unlike oil its mobility has, until recently, been restricted to those areas to which it could be moved by pipeline. In the United States its use is of nation-wide importance. In other areas where it occurs it can be of inestimable value to industry—as in northern Italy since the war and now, following the discovery of important deposits, probably in southern Italy and the Netherlands too. Recently, however, the transport of natural gas in liquid form in special vessels at very low temperatures has been developed, opening up new possibilities in the pattern of world demand and supply for fuels.

The main effects of oil as an energy source upon the location of industrial activity result naturally from its relative mobility. Oil has not in general attracted major industries to its source of origin, and where it has done so it has been as a raw material rather than as a source of energy. A good example is the large petro-chemical industry of the Gulf Coast of USA. But for a variety of reasons major industrial concentrations have not yet become a normal feature of oilfields as they have of coalfields. Since it is economically moved by pipeline and tanker, however, oil has played a part in the energy requirements of industry thousands of miles away and has still, if necessary, competed effectively with coal. Its triple role in location therefore has been, first, to permit a greater degree and variety of industrial development in locations away from coalfields, which were severely handicapped in the days of coal's monopoly; secondly, to permit a greater diversity of industry on the coalfields themselves; and thirdly, to provide the motive force for transport vehicles, especially in road transport, of which the importance has been indicated in Chapter 2.

Apart from the development of oil and natural gas as new primary sources of energy, the last decades of the nineteenth century also saw the reappearance in a new guise of man's ancient friend, water power, now to be used in the generation of electricity, and this is discussed in the following section.

Electricity and modern industry

The use of electricity has profoundly changed the structure and role of energy supplies in modern industry, and has had certain important consequences on the location of industrial activity. But the significant use of electricity dates only from the 1890's, and the most marked effects have been felt only in the past three or four decades. We must bear in mind also that electricity is just another way of utilising the major primary energy sources that we have already discussed, and it does not replace them. Neither does it provide a self-sufficient form of energy for industrial uses, but serves to extend the application of the primary sources over wider areas and over a wider range of industrial processes. It should be noted that giant steam turbines in large central stations (mainly using coal, including brown coal, but with growing use of fuel oil) provide nearly all of the existing world generating capacity. The tapping of the great potential of water power sites is of significance, causing some regions to experience 'an industrial development that would have been utterly inconceivable in 1870',[11] but this must not be over-stressed in the general picture.

For reasons that are readily understood, electricity has become a vital source of power for a wide range of modern industries. Over limited distances it is uniquely mobile, divorced from any pre-existing line of communication. It is also uniquely flexible in application, available at the flick of a switch, controlled at the turn of a knob. It calls for no storage facilities of any kind, thus saving capital investment in stocks, space and equipment in the individual firm. (This can be a disadvantage, too, for the firm is then at the mercy of an outside supply and has no reserves to call on in an emergency. The chances of a complete and prolonged breakdown of supply, however, are probably no greater than the chances of a prolonged strike affecting the supply of coal or fuel oil.) Technological advances have steadily broadened the field of industrial use for electricity. At the turn of the century most firms provided their own motive power from individual steam boilers, and the costs of the supply of coal for these was a significant consideration in the choice of location and site. Nowadays, the electric motor is the common means of motive power and the firm is no longer concerned with access to large quantities of coal, especially when its fuel requirements are also relatively small. Further, a number of new industries, including the electrical manufacturing industries themselves, have developed because of electric power.

Some of the most important of these involve processes that require enormous quantities of controlled energy, and these are naturally drawn to locations where such supplies are available at an attractive price—i.e. often to hydro-electric stations, despite the difficulties of remoteness and rugged terrain that are often associated with such locations.*

The industrial demand for electricity is therefore strong and growing rapidly. On the supply side, too, technical advances have greatly increased the efficiency of thermal electricity generating stations, as well as the ability of engineers to harness available water power. Such developments, in affecting the location of new generating capacity, have also affected the location of industry. But the field of technological progress charged with most possibilities for industrial location is that of electrical transmission. In the early 1880's Edison's first central electricity station in New York could transmit its low-voltage direct current over a radius of less than a mile from the point of generation. Subsequently the use of alternating current and the transformer permitted longer transmission distances, though still with substantial losses of energy. In 1891, for example, electricity was transmitted over 108 miles between two points in Germany, but with a loss of about 25 per cent of the original energy.[12] Thus, although transmission distances rose, they did not normally exceed about 30 miles in the 1890's. Niagara was operating in 1894 and sending electricity about 20 miles to Buffalo. Here also, it is interesting to note, we find electro-process industry being attracted to the power site as early as 1895. Aluminium reduction came first and shortly thereafter artificial abrasives, calcium carbide, graphite, electric steel and others.

In the present century the efficient range of transmission has advanced in step with the increasing range of uses. In the inter-war years great strides were made in power production and in the techniques of distribution, using voltages between 100,000 and 200,000 volts. The interconnection of separate sections of distribution network (in grid systems) permitted greater centralisation of power production in large plants at low-cost locations.[13] A grid system not only gives assured supplies in normal circumstances, but also provides substantial economies, since surplus capacity in

* Note, however, the increasing ability of well-located, modern, coal-fired power stations to meet this kind of demand. Thus the Ohio River area is becoming an increasingly important centre of aluminium smelting in USA, using power from coal-fired stations.

one area at any given time is available to other areas. A more even, regular and assured supply of electricity throughout a country or region offers further freedom to industry in its choice of location.

Meanwhile, the range of economic transmission of hydro-electric power has increased tremendously and has been largely associated with increases in the transmission voltage. In Sweden, for example, electricity generated at Harspranget is sent, at 380,000 volts alternating current, 600 miles to the south with only a 7 per cent loss in transmission. In Russia, energy is now being transmitted, at 400,000 volts alternating current, about 500 miles from the hydro-electricity station at Kuibischev to Moscow, while several countries are working or experimenting with even higher voltages.[14] Further extensions of transmission distances, with their consequent effects on industrial activity and potential, will probably depend on using very high voltage direct current, the many problems of which are being overcome. Technically it may shortly be possible to transmit large blocks of energy for more than a thousand miles, linking consuming centres with new and distant sources of electricity. The economic feasibility will depend upon the individual case, for costs of insulation and transformation rise with the voltage. In the USSR the incentive to develop transmission distances yet further is very great, for large but undeveloped coal resources and water power lie east of the Urals, remote (often 1,000 miles or more) from the main centres of industry. Elsewhere the possible rewards are also tremendous . . . 'the Congo might become the power house of Central Africa'.[15]

We have intimated that such advances in the field of production, utilisation and, above all, transmission of electric power are pregnant with possible repercussions in the realm of industrial location. It remains to inquire what effects the use of electricity has had so far. It is essential to remember that only some four or five decades have passed since electricity became a major form of industrial energy, and that its most developed use has been in countries which were already well advanced in their industrial economies before electricity became really important. Established centres of industry do not decline overnight and it is difficult as yet to assess adequately the locational impact of electric power in industry. Some electro-process industries have certainly been attracted to hydro-electricity stations where large blocks of electric power were available comparatively cheaply. Examples can be seen in the location of electro-chemical plant in Norway and of aluminium refining at Kitimat, British Columbia. But such locations, important though they are, have not yet developed into industrial concentrations of a size and importance even remotely comparable with the old coalfield and nodal locations. Indeed, the inadequacies of electric energy in meeting the full range of industrial requirements, including fuel as well as power, seem to indicate that centres possessing only electric energy from water power will not readily develop the wide range of industrial interests that are common in many older types of location, while, as has been intimated, new and highly efficient thermal power stations on developed coalfields are now proving attractive to large power-using industries.

An equally important feature of the industrial use of electricity is that its mobility not only enables power to be available in new locations, but also enables power to be supplied over long distances to old locations and centres of population. In this way therefore, the use of electricity may serve to reinforce existing patterns of location. Apart then from the electro-process industries, what effects has the use of electricity had on the rise of new locations? Again we emphasise that we are working from incomplete evidence because of the comparatively short span of time over which electricity has exercised whatever locational impulse it may have. Further, the advance of electricity has been contemporaneous with other important advances which have also served to loosen the bonds that in the nineteenth century tied much industrial capacity to certain locations. This is especially true of motor transport, which, like electricity, has had its greatest impact since the 1920's; while other advances in efficiency of utilisation of materials and energy sources (especially the wider use of oil), and the rise of new light industries have also tended over the same period to give many industrial concerns greater freedom in their choice of possible location. It is impossible fully to disentangle the locational effects of these separate influences.

Again, this greater degree of freedom which electricity, among other things, has conferred upon industry is permissive and not compulsive. In well-established industrial countries it does not by itself mean the rise of entirely new locations, for old centres retain such transport, market, labour and other advantages as they previously possessed. The effects of electric power supplies on location have therefore often been remarkably local. Factories have been enabled to move away from old sites where, among other things, coal was easily available—but this too has been aided by the other parallel advances mentioned above. In industrial cities this has meant, where it has meant anything at all, a move to a suburb, taking advantage of lower land values, the opportunity to develop a more spacious and productive lay-out and to offer local employment opportunities to suburban dwellers and so on, while retaining the many advantages of proximity to the large centre. It has not resulted in a major redistribution of national industrial capacity in any country and a widely held opinion that, for example, the growth of industrial capacity in south-east England of recent decades owes its existence to the use of electric power is, though not entirely false, a gross oversimplification. For many good reasons the south-east would have improved its national position anyway.

Electricity, therefore, might well permit the emergence of patterns of industrial location comprising small, scattered units, but in the absence of some impelling advantages associated with such a dispersal of industry there has been little tendency on the part of industry in general to avail itself of its freedom in this respect. In scattering industrial potential over a broad area various important economies of concentration would have to be foregone and, although some industries function more efficiently in small, dispersed centres, most apparently still prefer a location in a major industrial region and in, or on the fringe of, an established centre of some size. The industries that find a pattern of dispersed location an advantage would have found such a pattern equally advantageous had there been no development of electric power. General fuel economies, a wider use of oil, transport developments enabling coal and labour force to move longer distances and other such advances would probably have made their relative cost position as favourable as it is now.

In short, those movements towards dispersal of industry over large areas, as in the USA, that have occurred in recent decades were movements that, attracted by material, market, labour and other considerations, would probably have occurred anyway, and it would be misleading to ascribe them to the use of electricity, although its availability may have facilitated them. The main locational effects of the industrial use of electricity so far discernible are (i) in the location of electro-process industries; (ii) in permitting more industries to capitalise on market locations where local energy resources have become inadequate or expensive or are entirely lacking; and (iii) in conjunction with other advances helping to decrease the relative importance of energy considerations in location decisions, both regional and local.[16]

Energy and modern industry

So far we have discussed the various forms of energy, their respective advantages in industrial uses and their broad influence upon the location of industrial activity. We may recall that the changing impact of fuel and power supply on location considerations has been caused in large measure by the possibility of substituting one energy source for another, and it may now be useful to present the changing picture in statistical form. In this we use total energy consumption for all purposes and assume that industrial energy consumption changes in approximately the same proportions. This is justified by the nature of available statistics, the broadness of the purpose in mind and the fact that in advanced industrial economies well over half the total energy consumption is in industrial and transport uses—some two-thirds in the United Kingdom and about three-quarters in the United States, for example.

Through much of the nineteenth century coal virtually monopolised the energy supply situation and, although in the earlier decades the direct use of water power was still important in certain areas, it was steadily declining. Available statistics are incomplete and unreliable, but by 1880 it has been estimated that coal provided about 97 per cent of a total world energy supply of about 319 million tons of coal equivalent. In 1900 the proportion was still 94 per cent out of a total of some 778 million. In both years oil and natural gas provided all but a tiny fraction of the remainder.[17] Table 2 shows the position in recent decades. It should be noted that the decline of coal is relative and that for the world as a whole there has as yet been no absolute decline in coal consumption. Coal still meets nearly half the total world energy requirements, but this world average masks wide regional differences. Table 3 illustrates this. The United Kingdom and Belgium represent 'coal economies' and, though the use of oil has grown rapidly during and since the period shown, coal remains the basic energy source. Norway and Sweden represent the 'water power economies'. In both, hydro-electricity naturally takes pride of place,* but the many advantages possessed by oil—plus the decade or more of serious coal shortage in Europe following the

* The basis of the conversion of hydro power to coal equivalents used here may favour hydro-electricity. See footnote to Table 2.

TABLE 2

WORLD PRIMARY ENERGY CONSUMPTION BY TYPE

Selected years

Per cent of total

Year	Coal and lignite	Oil	Natural gas	Hydro-electricity	Total in million metric tons coal equivalent
1929	76	14	4	5	1,799
1937	71	17	6	6	1,928
1950	59	24	10	7	2,677
1954	51	29	11	8	3,215
1958	50	28	13	9	3,984
1962	46	31	15	8	4,868

Source: United Nations, Statistical Papers, series J, nos. 1–7. (Percentage figures do not always total to 100, because of rounding)

Note: The relative position of hydro-electric power in the table depends upon the basis of conversion of electric power to coal equivalents. In this table the coal equivalent of hydro-electricity is based on the quantities of coal required, at prevailing efficiencies, to generate 1,000 kwh, i.e. 0·6 metric tons. In the later UN, series J, publications, however, the basis of conversion became a coefficient based on the quantity of heat energy that could be produced under ideal conditions. On this basis 1,000 kwh = 0·125 metric tons of coal, and the proportions of world consumption for 1958, for e.g., would be as follows: coal and lignite 54%; oil 31%; natural gas 14%; hydro-electricity 1%

second world war—have resulted in petroleum products displacing coal as the chief imported energy source. The United States represents an economy where all the primary sources are available, and the table tells its own story here. Denmark represents an economy with little or no native energy resources and here again petroleum imports have gained substantially.

To a large extent, therefore (and apart from unpredictable results of government policies), the pattern of energy supply to industry will depend on the resource endowment of the region, the possibility of its economic exploitation and the position of the region relative to outside sources. This will be reflected in both the type and the location of industrial activity. The general trend clearly discernible from the tables is towards a greater use of petroleum and, where possible, natural gas, plus the greater

Source: OEEC, Industrial Statistics 1900–55, table 23 and UN, series J, no. 7. The hydro-electricity consumption for 1962 has been converted to coal equivalents on the same basis as the OEEC table, i.e. 1,000 kwh=0·6 metric tons of coal

TABLE 3

NATIONAL VARIATIONS IN SOURCES OF ENERGY CONSUMED

Selected countries for selected years

Percentage of total

Country	Coal and lignite			Petroleum products			Natural gas			Hydro-electricity			Total consumption in millions metric tons coal equivalent		
	1929	1950	1962	1929	1950	1962	1929	1950	1962	1929	1950	1962	1929	1950	1962
United Kingdom	96	91	71	4	9	27	—	—	(0·05)	—	—	2	188	223	269
Belgium–Lux.	99	91	71	1	9	29	—	—	—	—	—	—	38	31	42
Norway	35	13	4	4	13	18	—	—	—	61	74	78	8	14	29
Sweden	65	31	7	7	23	44	—	—	—	28	46	49	10	23	47
United States	66	40	23	22	33	38	9	22	33	3	1	6	793	1,140	1,624
Denmark	90	72	36	10	27	59	—	—	—	—	1	5	6	9	16

(Totals out because of rounding)

development of hydro-electric potential. Coal no longer dominates so completely the energy supply situation and has consequently lost much of its direct attraction to industry. An increasing number of industries has become progressively able to choose from among two, three and sometimes four possible sources of energy. Other things being equal, the locational influence of any *one* is therefore bound to be reduced.

A similar influence has been exercised by steadily increasing efficiency in energy utilisation. Palmer Putnam tentatively estimates[18] that the aggregate efficiency in the use of energy over the world as a whole in 1860 was 10·5 per cent. He gives efficiencies at that time as about 8 per cent in the United Kingdom and United States, 10 per cent in Germany, 12 per cent in France and 5 per cent in India. For 1950 he estimates the world aggregate efficiency at about 22 per cent, with the United States at 30 per cent, the United Kingdom at 24 per cent, Germany and France at 20 per cent each and India at 6 per cent. These figures are based on general energy utilisation, and it is likely that efficiency has improved at a much faster rate in industrial than in other uses. The effects of such improvements in efficiency have again been, understandably, to decrease the importance of fuel and power in location decisions.

There have, therefore, been three broad sets of forces at work influencing, within the framework of a continuous increase in total demand, the role of energy supplies in industrial activity. First, we have an increasing element of choice as between alternative primary sources, which has tended to decrease the locational 'pull' of any one source. Second, we have steadily improving efficiency in utilisation, which tends to decrease the relative importance of energy considerations. Third, there is the rise to positions of outstanding importance of many new industries and processes for which energy requirements are a minor consideration. Each new discovery or innovation has served to weaken the physical ties that limited the possible choice of location. Whether the processes thus liberated took advantage of their greater locational freedom or not is another matter, affected by a host of separate considerations. What *has* been a common feature is the decreasing relative costs of fuel and power in industrial processes and consequently a decreasing importance of energy *per se* in the bulk of location decisions.

Some statistical measure of the relative importance of fuel and power in different industries will now be helpful. Table 4 (p. 63)

TABLE 4

COSTS OF FUELS AND PURCHASED ENERGY AS A PERCENTAGE OF VALUE ADDED BY MANUFACTURE
USA 1962

Selected industry groups and industries

A Industry groups	%	B Individual industries	%
All industries	3·5	Lime	30·0
Primary metal industries	10·0	Primary zinc*	27·2
Stone, clay and glass products	8·4	Primary aluminium	24·7
Paper and allied products	6·5	Cement, hydraulic	22·6
Chemicals and allied products	5·9	Inorganic chemicals	20·6
Textile mill products	3·7	Brick and structural tile*	19·4
Food and kindred products	2·9	Electro-metallurgical products=	17·0
Non-electrical machinery	1·6	Pulp mills	14·9
Transport equipment	1·5	Blast furnaces and steel mills	12·2
Electrical machinery	1·3	Glass containers	8·7
Printing and publishing	1·0		

Source: US Annual Survey of Manufactures, 1962

* From Census of Manufactures, 1958

expresses the costs of fuels and purchased energy as a percentage of the value added by manufacture in selected industry groups and industries in the United States in 1962. A cautionary note is essential. Large energy consumers will be especially concerned to locate at a point where energy supplies can be obtained cheaply. Much effort will have been applied to the problem of reducing energy costs. The manufacture of carbon black, for example, is strongly attracted to locations where power is cheaply available but, largely through careful location, the ratio of energy costs to value added by manufacture is below 5 per cent in the United States. Large fuel and power users normally figure relatively high in a table of fuel costs, however, and Table 4 is useful for the general purpose in mind, though it is risky to use the figures for detailed comparisons of the importance of fuel and power supplies in location decisions.

The table shows that over all industries fuel and power costs averaged about 3·5 per cent of value added by manufacture in 1962. There has been a steady decrease in this figure since the beginning of the century. The U.S. Census of 1909 shows a ratio of just under 7 per cent, which by 1939 had fallen to 5·3 per cent and by 1947 to 4·5 per cent. This illustrates the decreasing general importance of energy costs to industry for the reasons outlined in the previous paragraphs. The significances of 'new' industries may be emphasised at this point. The non-electrical machinery, the electrical machinery and the transport equipment groups (Table 4, column A) contain many of the new twentieth-century industrial products. Together they provided almost 30 per cent of total value added by manufacture in the United States in 1962 and in all of them the ratio of energy costs to value added is under 2 per cent.

Table 4, column B, lists a few manufacturing processes in which the ratio of energy costs to value added by manufacture is relatively high. In these, every effort will have been made to reduce energy costs, while keeping other important considerations in view. This last qualification is important. High fuel and power costs do not necessarily mean that a location must be chosen close to fuel and power supplies. It will mean a deep concern with the varying costs of energy supply in alternative locations, but it may be even more essential to satisfy other requirements as, for example, access to raw materials or markets. We saw in Chapter 2 that the location of steel works can be strongly influenced by the structure of freight rates, which may, as at present in the United States, strongly favour the movement of fuel and raw materials rather than the finished product. Thus a location at the market becomes increasingly attractive to steel mills and, because of the great economies achieved by integration, to blast furnaces also. The relatively high fuel and energy costs in iron production are, therefore, not entirely reflected in location. Cement manufacture is a good example of an industry in which fuel and energy costs are very high, but in which other requirements, especially access to markets, may be decisive in location decisions. In such enterprises fuel and power requirements, though large, must be put into perspective.

We may distinguish three broad categories of industry based on the possible role of energy supplies in the location decision. Our first category contains many industries in which fuel and power costs are of relatively little importance in location—provided general supply conditions are adequate and reliable, as they are in most advanced economies. In these industries the quantities used are relatively small or, if considerable, access to markets or to raw materials is of much greater significance. Most of the processes in the industrial groups at the bottom of Table 4, column A, are of this kind. Among the larger energy consumers also in this class is the manufacture of ice which, though requiring large quantities of electric power, must be located close to its market.

At the opposite end of the scale there are the relatively few processes where energy supplies remain a dominant consideration in location. This is the case in the carbon black industry, mentioned above, and the primary aluminium industry, as well as in other electro-metallurgical and electro-chemical processes.

Between these two come a whole range of processes in which fuel and power costs may influence the location choice in varying degrees, depending on the strength of other influences. From Table 4, column B, we may select such examples as blast furnaces and steel works, the cement, brick and structural tile, paper pulp and glass container industries, in all of which raw material procurement or the marketing of the product must be weighed against energy supplies. Because of the advances in supply, transport and use of energy to which we have several times referred, the influence of fuel and power supplies on this group of industries has declined greatly and is still declining.

Although the part played by energy supplies in industrial location decisions at the present time should not, therefore, be over-stressed, certain important effects are still strongly in evidence, quite apart from the power-oriented industries. The energy

c

supply situation in any area (reflected in the price of fuel and power) will influence the type of industrial economy. The effects on industrial structure of the possession of hydro-electric potential alone as a primary energy source were intimated above. It remains to mention the case of the region that is relatively badly endowed with major primary energy sources and in which the relative price of fuel and power is high. Such a region will not be an attractive location to any industry where fuel and power requirements are much above average—unless it possesses some other positive advantage, or group of advantages, which will more than offset higher fuel and power costs. Few regions labouring under such a basic deficiency would ever grow to important status industrially. An important example of relatively high energy prices is, however, to be found in New England. Here in the early stages of industrialisation the water power resources were attractive to industrialists. Subsequently they proved to be inadequate and, although New England remains an important centre of industrial activity, its industrial structure has been affected, for the larger fuel and power consuming industries can play only a small part in this region. This is a serious disadvantage, for among the industries with large energy requirements are some key industries by proximity to which many secondary industries stand to gain significant economies. Many users of iron and steel, for example, can economise by a location close to an iron and steel works. But a New England location would place a modern blast furnace and steel works at a distinct competitive disadvantage in its fuel costs, a disadvantage which would not be offset by sufficiently strong compensatory advantages. This applies also to other large energy consumers and the industrial structure of New England shows the dominance of industries which use relatively little fuel and power. In consequence, despite high fuel and power prices, the overall ratio of fuel and power costs to value added by manufacture in New England is only 2·7 per cent as compared with the national ratio of 3·5 per cent.

This example stresses again the importance of early developments to existing locations. Although access to and costs of energy supplies are now no longer dominant location features for most industries, much of the existing geographical pattern of industry was laid down when they were. This indeed is why throughout the industrial world coalfields became and have remained major centres of industrial activity. The manifold acquired advantages of such areas ensure that they remain important.

Nuclear energy and other innovations

Finally, it is perhaps desirable to discuss briefly the possible locational effects of innovations in energy supply. Much research is being directed to the development of other primary sources of energy. We may consider first the relatively minor fields of development of solar, wind, tidal and geothermal energy and the thermal energy of the sea. Apart from geothermal energy such sources are permanent, but for solar, wind and tidal energy, they are intermittent. In the absence of inexpensive storage mechanisms they are of limited present value and cannot be attractive to any important level of industrial development. Moreover, the location of sites of exploitation would not in general permit these sources to be of much value to existing centres of industry. The most significant application of these primary sources would be in the form of electricity (although some non-electrical applications may be possible as in heating, refrigeration, mechanical power and solar furnaces) which might have to compete with power generated from conventional sources. Although there may be regions where such energy forms could make a limited contribution in the nearer future (long-term possibilities could be greater), we may assume that they will have no immediate impact on the location of industry.[19]

Of much greater concern are the possible effects of nuclear energy applications. Nuclear power stations use uranium or thorium as fuel, but they use them so efficiently that fuel costs will become a minor factor in the supply of power from nuclear stations. The small quantities of fuel required make the nuclear station independent of fuel transport costs in its location. But, although stations may be located without reference to fuel transport considerations (political and strategic problems aside), they are not entirely free from all physical ties, for site requirements are quite stringent. Moreover, while fuel costs are low, capital costs are at present extremely high. This fact, alongside that of great advances in 'conventional' generation,[20] means that electricity generated by nuclear stations is not yet fully competitive in price with that generated by conventional stations. There has been much speculation on the possible role of nuclear power in underdeveloped countries, but the high capital costs alone may put a significant level of development of nuclear energy out of the reach of most under-developed areas for the present. Indeed, such areas often possess significant reserves of conventional primary energy which, because of capital shortage among other things, remain largely unexploited. The estimates of eventual ability of nuclear power stations to complete with coal or oil fired stations are also based on the assumption that the nuclear plant will be a base load station, selling most of its large output all the time. Not every region has the ability to absorb such large quantities of electric power continuously, although it is now thought that nuclear stations with small outputs may eventually become feasible technically and economically.

For such reasons the impact of nuclear energy on industrial location may not be great in the immediate future. The present method of application is to use the heat generated by nuclear fission to heat a gas (or eventually a liquid), which in turn heats water to raise steam to drive turbines. In short it is another way of producing electricity and merely introduces another element of choice into the decision from which primary source to generate power. The impact of its low fuel costs, besides being offset by high capital costs, may also be restricted by the fact that transmission and distribution costs (which form a substantial proportion of the total) will be the same as for a conventional station on the same site. In any case electric power does not, as we have seen, provide a self-sufficient form of energy for industry as a whole, while energy costs are generally small, and a declining factor in most location decisions. As Isard and Whitney point out,[21] even zero energy costs might have little locational implications, probably serving in the main to increase the application of power in place of labour in old and new processes in existing locations.

One interesting field of possible development might be to increase the practice of refining ores at their source, thus saving transfer costs on waste material. Alternatively one stage in the processing of a raw material (the stage that is now often attracted to a hydro-electric power site) could be re-located at the final market for the product. The aluminium industry is an example, but many considerations other than power are involved.[22]

In the absence of any revolutionary new techniques of applying nuclear energy to industrial processes, the locational impact will in all probability not be remarkable in the present century. It seems likely that, in the short run, it will serve mainly to supplement the conventional power sources in advanced industrial communities.

[1] A. Parker, 'Man's Use of Solar Energy', *Advancement of Science*, vol. VII, no. 28, 1951

[2] Ibid.

[3] J. H. Dales, 'Fuel, Power and Industrial Development in Central Canada', *American Economic Review*, vol. XLIII, no. 2, May 1953

[4] E. J. Cohn, *Industry in the Pacific North West and Location Theory*, 1954 pp. 113 ff.

[5] W. H. K. Turner, 'The Significance of Water Power in Industrial Location', *Scottish Geographical Magazine*, vol. LXXIV, no. 2, September 1958

[6] For details see V. S. Clarke, *Manufacturing in the United States*, vol. I, *1607–1860*, 1916

[7] Ibid., vol. II, *1860 1914*, 1928, pp. 533 ff.

[8] A. P. Usher, *A History of Mechanical Inventions*, 1954, chapter XV. The present requirement is about one-third of the mid-1920's level.

[9] H. Cunliffe, *The Times Review of Industry*, May 1959

[10] Ibid.

[11] Usher, op. cit., p. 404

[12] Clarke, op. cit., p. 380

[13] For examples in the UK see E. M. Rawstron in *Geography*, 1951 (pp. 249–62) and 1955 (pp. 92–7)

[14] See J. H. Sykes, *The Times Review of Industry*, November 1959, and September 1964

[15] The Earl of Verulam and others, 'The Geography of Power. Its Sources and Transmission', *Geographical Journal*, September 1952. There is already a plan to bring power, at 900,000 volts DC, from water power sites in Labrador to New York—a distance of about 1,000 miles. Sykes, op. cit., September 1964

[16] An important study of this general subject of electricity and industry is made in J. H. Dales, *Hydroelectricity and Industrial Development—Quebec 1898–1940*, 1957

[17] W. S. and E. S. Woytinsky, *World Population and Production*, p. 930. The basis of conversion to coal equivalents used here differs somewhat from that used in Tables 2 and 3

[18] Palmer Putnam, *Energy in the Future*, 1954, p. 90

[19] See United Nations, Department of Economic and Social Affairs, *New Sources of Energy and Economic Development*, 1957

[20] Since the mid-1950's, forecasts of dates by which nuclear power would be as cheap as 'conventional' power have been consistently falsified by the advances made in the design, building and operation of coal and oil fired stations. The following are the estimated costs per kwh for three stations due for commissioning in the UK in 1966: Oldbury (nuclear) 0.72*d*., (0.49 capital charges, 0·23 running costs); Eggborough (coal) 0·50*d*., (0·12 capital charges, 0·38 running costs); Fawley (oil) 0·54*d*. (0·12 capital charges, 0·42 running costs). *The Times Review of Technology and Industry*, February 1965. (Note, however, that the relative running costs for coal and oil stations are affected by the duty that has to be paid on oil imports—a duty designed to protect the coal industry)

[21] W. Isard and V. Whitney, *Atomic Power. An Economic and Social Analysis*, 1952. An excellent treatment of energy and industrial location.

[22] See Isard and Whitney, op. cit., chapter VI

Note: Since the first edition of this book G. Manners has published *The Geography of Energy* in this series (1964)—a detailed, highly recommended study

4

THE INFLUENCE OF THE
FACTORS OF PRODUCTION

So far we have dealt with those influences in which the costs of movement can prove of importance. There are many processes, however, for which the costs of assembling the materials, of obtaining fuel and power supplies and distributing the products provide a low, or even negligible, percentage of total costs, given the existence of a satisfactory transport service. In these circumstances the relative costs of processing at various locations may become of greater importance than the considerations we have already outlined. Various influences affect processing costs in any given location. Normally they do not act in isolation, but in conjunction with other issues they serve to make one location more attractive than others from a cost point of view. Thus labour costs are important in most productive enterprises and may sometimes be predominant. Physical proximity to 'linked' industries may be essential for efficient production in some industries. Further, the availability of capital, the types of sites and services available locally, local taxes, government activity, all these elements and many more may have to be weighed in the attempt to decide which location will permit maximum economies in production. The 'ideal' location for any given enterprise probably does not exist, but the intelligent entrepreneur will seek, as far as possible, the particular combination of favourable features that most nearly meets his individual needs. If several possible locations appear equally attractive, the final decision may be affected by a feature of little intrinsic importance. For convenience of exposition the various elements in the situation are separated. In this chapter we shall discuss only the factors of production.

The factors of production are labour, capital[1] and enterprise, all of which are available to industry at a price. The price paid for the use of these factors (termed respectively wages, interest and profits) naturally enters into the total costs of production. This price varies geographically for a number of reasons, the most important being the imperfect mobility of the factors of production. If they were perfectly mobile, then geographical differences in their price would virtually disappear. For example, if the returns on similar types of capital investment at point X were higher than at point Y, and capital were perfectly mobile between these two areas, then capital would be transferred from Y to X, thus raising the 'price' of capital at Y and lowering it at X until the two areas were in equilibrium. In fact labour, capital and enterprise are very far from being perfectly mobile and, for this and other reasons, geographical differences will exist in the price that has to be paid for the use of each factor.

To some extent these variations in factor price can be offset by varying the proportions in which they are utilised. This means that the scarcer and more expensive factor of production is used more intensively. Thus, if capital is the most expensive item, it can be used more intensively by increasing the application of labour to a given piece of capital equipment, e.g. by working it for two or three shifts. If labour is the most expensive, the tendency will be to employ more capital per unit of labour and so on. In conditions of perfect competition the equilibrium, or most economic, situation would be reached when the marginal unit of production of any factor is equal to that of any other, having regard to the price of each factor. This can be stated as a simple equation:

$$\frac{\text{Marginal product of factor A}}{\text{Price of factor A}} = \frac{\text{Marginal product of factor B}}{\text{Price of factor B}}$$

$$= \frac{\text{Marginal product of factor Z}}{\text{Price of factor Z}}$$

If the actual situation does not approximate to this theoretical equilibrium, it will pay the producer to use more of the factor of production for which the marginal product divided by its price is greatest, until they all become equal. The most efficient combination (the least cost combination) of factors of production therefore takes into account the variations in the relative prices of those factors in different areas. By skilfully varying the inputs of the factors of production, some geographical variations in factor

prices can be, at least partially, offset. The value of skilled entrepreneurial juggling in this way should not be over-stressed, for
some variations may be of too great a magnitude to be erased by
varying the proportions. Certain locations will still possess advantages in processing a given commodity, even from a factor price
point of view.

It should also be noted that geographical variations in the prices
of (or rates paid for) the factors of production are not the only or
even the main consideration. Equally important in determining
the final processing costs are the geographical variations in productivity of those factors. In plain language this means that what
is important to the employer is not what he pays for the labour,
the management or the capital he uses, but what he gets for what
he pays. It is cheaper, for example, to pay an employee £5 a day
and get £6 worth of work from him than to pay £1 a day and get
15s. worth of work. Such variations in productivity can be attributed partially, perhaps, to natural conditions (e.g. type of
climate), but they chiefly arise from a whole complex of economic
and social causes. The efficiency and, therefore, the productivity
of labour, capital and enterprise in productive operations can vary
widely with differences in such conditions. We now consider each
factor in turn.

Labour

A supply of labour is naturally fundamental to all manufacturing
processes, but the weightiness of labour considerations in location
decisions varies widely from industry to industry. Even among
those industries where transfer costs do not play a leading part
(i.e. the industries that are not pulled almost inevitably to material
sources or to their markets) labour considerations are by no
means always paramount. In some industries, however, though
they are probably declining in number, the final product contains
a large element of labour cost in its total cost, and in such industries geographical differences in labour costs may remain
predominant in location. Such processes include those where techniques are not highly mechanised and the product thus has a high
labour component. Labour-saving devices, of great importance in
most modern industries, may not be well developed or, if existing,
are not being applied. Even in an advanced economy the least-
cost combination of factors may still favour labour in some
industries. Calculations from the US Annual Survey of Manufactures, 1962, show that total payroll costs then accounted for

24 per cent of the value of the goods despatched from manufacturing establishments in the country as a whole. A few examples of different industries illustrate, however, how widely the proportion of labour costs varies from one industry to another (Table 5).

TABLE 5

LABOUR COSTS AS A PROPORTION OF THE VALUE OF SHIPMENTS OF SELECTED INDUSTRIES, USA 1962

	%		%
Optical instrument and lens	44	All manufacturing	24
Metal cutting machine tool	41	Steel rolling and finishing	22
Computing machines, etc.	39	Paperboard	19
Millinery	34	Paints and varnishes	17
Footwear (ex. rubber)	32	Basic chemicals	16
Cutlery, handtools, etc.	30	Motor vehicles and parts	11
Women's dresses	27	Meat packing	9
Jewellery (precious metal)	27	Flour and meal	6
Cotton weaving	26	Petroleum refining	6

Source: Annual Survey of Manufactures, 1962

These figures are not necessarily typical of individual firms within each industry, nor do they necessarily indicate labour-oriented industries. But, clearly, labour considerations are likely to play a greater part in the location of optical instrument and lens manufacture than in meat packing plants.

The labour input is usually relatively high in the textile industries, the clothing and shoe industries and some engineering processes. Establishments in these industries are often relatively small and tend to employ a high percentage of female labour. When fashion products are involved, as in ladies' clothes manufacture, the firm may be tied securely to a centre of relatively high wages such as London or New York. In other branches of the clothing industry the manufacturer is sensitive to wage differentials in his choice of location. Thus ready-to-wear apparel factories and knitting mills have a wider distribution than the more fashion-conscious branches. A high percentage of labour costs is also found among firms producing luxury goods, such as jewellery, which cannot be subjected to mass-production techniques or move to areas of low wages. Further, products which still require manual skill of a high order (as in fine metal work) or which are ordered in specialist batches for particular customers also have a high labour component. Many small firms in Sheffield, for instance, produce special items to meet small orders, a condition that makes a high degree of standardisation and other techniques of mass-production inapplicable. In such industries, therefore, labour requirements strongly influence location decisions. But, even where labour is not of comparable importance, as in vehicle manufacture or oil refining, few firms will be indifferent to labour considerations, and we must analyse those features of the situation that may affect all firms in varying degrees. These features are essentially interdependent, but for purposes of discussion may be considered separately as follows:

1. Geographical variations in labour costs.
2. Geographical variations in labour supply.
3. The geographical distribution of labour with specific skills.

These regional variations owe their existence to the relative immobility of labour, both between areas and between jobs. The impediments to *geographical mobility* of labour are much less serious in advanced than in under-developed areas, but everywhere labour must be considered, in the short run at least, to be relatively immobile. We should in this context distinguish between 'local' and 'regional' mobility. In the advanced economy the development of suburban train, bus and private car commuting has greatly increased local mobility. Entrepreneurs can regard a wide area as a possible 'catchment basin' for labour, for people regularly travel twenty, thirty or even more miles from their home to their place of work. This is very significant locally, but we are more concerned in this part of our argument with inter-regional mobility, which requires the permanent uprooting of homes and the severing of local connections. Such movement is normally a slow process. Great migrations of population may follow some social, economic or political upheaval, but the flood dies away to a comparative trickle in 'normal' circumstances. The enormous population movements that followed both the second world war in Europe and the partition of the Indian sub-continent, for example, arose out of political circumstances, and much of it was compulsory. Of course, voluntary movements of large numbers of people do also occur, and are of great significance. The population of California, for example, grew by over 5 million (49 per cent) and that of Florida by over 2 million (79 per cent) between 1950 and 1960. Migration accounted for 61 per cent and 74 per cent respectively of these rapid increases, which have been caused by a complex of social and economic circumstances. While this may be regarded as evidence of high labour mobility, however, the fact remains that this mobility is not sufficient to equalise the price of labour of similar skills over large areas. The frictions opposing labour mobility remain important, even in USA, and preserve wide regional wage rate differentials which still play some part in location decisions.

Inter-industry mobility is also important in industrial societies, which are dynamic entities with growing and declining sectors. Labour released by contracting industry should, ideally, be absorbed smoothly elsewhere. In practice there is inevitably some friction here also, since cycles of growth and decline rarely mesh smoothly in a given geographical area and the skills required in one industry are not always suitable in others. The problem is made yet more difficult by the marked reluctance of many workers to change either their place of employment or their type of work. In a study of the employment history of a number of people after discharge from cotton mills, W. A. Miernik found that no fewer than 35 per cent found another textile-mill job. Few of the workers in his sample found employment in the expanding industries of their region (New England) . . . 'The displaced textile workers exhibited a remarkably low degree of inter-industry mobility. We also found relatively little evidence of geographical mobility among the workers included in our survey.'[2] Perhaps the first observation depended largely on the second, the workers being reluctant to move to where new jobs were available. A conditioning factor was no doubt to be found in the age structure of the discharged workers, most of whom tended to be in the higher age groups, 58 per cent being forty-six years old or more and only 2·5 per cent being below twenty-five. Nevertheless the study suggests that there is considerable short-term immobility of labour both between jobs and between areas. Other interesting examples of a different nature occur elsewhere. In Japan there has traditionally been a strong element of paternalism in the employer-employee relationship, and the idea that the employee had a life-long contract with his employer has militated against labour mobility and affected the growth and expansion of new enterprises. In general, immobility between industries serves to slow down, or prevent, the emergence of new 'growing points' in an industrial economy, and can lead to much avoidable hardship.

In the light of these circumstances a firm will normally wish to find an adequate pool of the kinds of labour it requires already existing in a prospective location. There may often be a steady internal migratory movement (especially from country to town as economics progress), but it is unlikely that this could normally affect the labour supply situation rapidly enough to influence a location decision. By locating in an area already provided with a pool of labour the employer also finds the essential social capital, e.g. housing, water supplies, sanitation services, schools, public transport services and so on, already in existence, a very important consideration. In special circumstances plant construction in a new location may precede the necessary labour supply, but from a purely economic point of view this is extravagant in capital requirements. It may, however, be necessary to construct plant in advance of labour supply in undeveloped areas. Here the assembly of the labour force at the site must often perforce await the prior provision of employment, homes and other social capital equipment. This raises the initial capital requirements greatly and is justified only by the special circumstances. The establishment of the aluminium industry at Kitimat, British Columbia, is a case in point. So also was the construction of the chemical fertiliser factory at Sindri in India, which commenced production in 1952. The initial capital requirements were very high indeed, far exceeding those for the construction of identical plant in a developed area. Not only had the factory and its equipment to be built and installed, but also road and rail communications had to be provided and a town constructed for the workers, with amenities such as schools, hospitals and markets.

We must, then, conclude that, in the short run at least, labour is an immobile factor of production. This being the case, geographical differences in labour supply, skills and costs do exist and do influence the location of industry. We now turn to examine these geographical variations in greater detail.

Labour cost variations are not entirely, or even mainly, a question of differing wage levels. High wage rates are not in themselves disadvantageous. Of equal or greater importance are such factors as labour attitudes, turn-over, absenteeism and the possibility of having to compete with other firms in the vicinity for available labour, all directly affecting productivity. Labour attitudes are very important. It is not unusual for militant trade unions to become well established in older industrial areas, and their activities sometimes cause worker-management relations to become very strained. Such an environment may not be attractive to firms seeking a new location, while existing firms may consider the possibility and desirability of opening branch plants in areas where labour attitudes are more favourable. From that point it is not unknown for firms to transfer gradually their major centre of production to the new location and, if times become difficult, the plant in the older centre may well be the first to be closed or have its activity reduced. Such considerations have been important in the recent rapid growth of industry in the south-east of USA and in the absolute or relative decline of certain industries in New England. In *Why Industry Moves South*, McLaughlin and Robock, examining the reasons for the location decisions of eighty-eight firms, show that almost without exception the firms concerned made a thorough study of the history of labour-management relations in the areas they were considering before they made a final decision. In some cases a discouraging labour record caused an otherwise favourable location to be rejected. Similarly in the United Kingdom the general tendency for new industry to grow in the southern parts of the country in the inter-war period was explained, in part, by the entrepreneurs' feeling that labour relations were easier in the south than in the centres of extremely heavy unemployment on the major coalfields.

Labour attitudes are naturally reflected in many ways, but most significantly in productivity. For example, in old-established industries a tradition concerning the proper amount of work for each individual to undertake is apt to grow up. An increase in this 'work load' is often strongly opposed. Even though technical advance makes it possible, for example, for one man to look after several machines, his union may refuse to accept a change in the previous work assignment. Such opposition to innovation is of course no new thing in human affairs. It has probably played a part in hastening the inevitable decline of the Lancashire cotton industry.

The size of town is also found to affect labour costs, and not only because of the wage differential that is often found to exist between large and small centres. Although a large town itself possesses many advantages, some firms favour smaller centres where, they maintain, certain other labour cost advantages exist apart from the slightly lower wage level. Such added advantages include a lower rate of labour turnover (there being fewer alternative jobs available), lower rates of absenteeism and generally favourable labour attitudes. But to be a big fish in a little pool can also bring difficulties. With reference here only to the labour situation, there is less freedom in recruiting workers and terminating their employment than in a large centre.

A final consideration in labour costs may be summed up in the term 'fringe benefits', the necessity to contribute to these varying from region to region. Contributions by the firm to welfare schemes, insurance schemes, provision of canteen and recreational facilities and so on can add substantially to total labour expenses.[3] It must be repeated, however, that the true cost of labour is not measured by what the employer has to pay, but by what he gets for what he pays, and high outgoings on account of labour may result, in a well managed firm with a labour force of good quality, in low cost per unit of output.

So much for labour costs *per se*. Geographical variations in labour supply are also significant. They are directly reflected in the organisation of industrial undertakings and may be reflected in costs. Large labour concentrations are often very attractive to industry, for in a large population an industrialist is more likely to find the particular types of worker that suit his needs best, while his labour supply is more flexible and organisations exist through which he can quickly obtain more workers. He can also lay off workers without the difficulty that may accompany such a decision in a small or one-industry town. An example of the latter difficulty can be taken from Australia, where, at Broken Hill, many employees made redundant by a decline in demand for lead in 1958 and 1959 were carried on the companies' pay roll because there was no alternative employment available in the town. Large labour concentrations also provide a market for the manufacturer of consumer goods, a location feature of high importance.

Labour supply considerations do not embrace only the physical existence of labour. The type of labour is also important, its age and sex structure, the level of industrial capability and so on. Male and female labour are usually in 'joint supply'; that is, where there is the one the other will often be available. Thus an area with industries employing a large percentage of males may well be a favourable place to establish an industry employing mainly female labour. In the USA such a situation is held to be the original cause of the location of the silk and rayon industries in the east Pennsylvanian anthracite region, for example at Scranton and Wilkes Barre.

In most advanced industrial areas an essential minimum of

technical and industrial 'know how' is a common possession of the population, and industry can draw upon a large pool of satisfactory labour. Reared in an industrial environment labour adapts itself comparatively readily to the various requirements of industrial work. Apart from special skills (which are mentioned separately below) the workers can quickly understand and operate new machines and adopt new processes (labour attitudes permitting). Generally the training period will be short for the majority of jobs in industry The situation is, however, greatly different in the under-developed areas, where labour supply for industry is a major problem. Here even the most basic elements of industrial 'know how' are often lacking, and industrial life is completely foreign to the vast majority of people. In such circumstances the knowledge of even the simplest of industrial techniques is not available among a prospective labour force, training periods are long, labour turnover is rapid and damage rates are very high. Thus efficiency of labour is generally low and labour costs high, even though wage rates are low. Such an environment is quite unsatisfactory for many manufacturing processes, but the low wage rates may be an advantage for certain simple industries. The cotton textile industry, for example, is one in which the techniques of production of low-grade cloths, for which there is a large market, can be relatively quickly acquired. The machinery is relatively robust, and satisfactory conditions of production can be established within a comparatively short time. For industries that are not so amenable, however, labour shortcomings render under-developed areas unsatisfactory, though not necessarily impossible.

An example from India will show the kind of difficulty that such labour conditions may produce, but at the same time indicate how they can sometimes be overcome. In India wages rates are in general only about one-fifth of those current in western Europe, and we might therefore expect Indian manufacturers to make lavish use of labour and relatively little use of capital. This is often the case, but some new industrial plants in India contain more automatic machinery, designed to save labour, than some of the works of their European competitors. The explanation of this apparent anomaly lies in the fact that in India the supply of skilled labour, machinists and fitters for example, is extremely short. That is the core of the matter, but in addition firms may be compelled by law to provide housing and other services, which indirectly raise further the real costs of labour. Firms therefore often have a strong incentive to find ways and means of keeping their labour force small, despite the low rate of wages. The labour conditions of the country are on balance a handicap to India as compared with western Europe and act as a brake, though not the only one, on the rapid development of the manufacturing industries the country so badly needs.

Labour supply is also affected by outside factors of a legal or organisational nature. The inter-industry mobility, which we have seen to be of importance in an advanced economy, can be restricted by union activity, for example, by the operation of the 'closed shop'. Unions may also impose certain conditions that affect the supply of labour by insisting on an out-dated apprenticeship system and so on. Legal restrictions on the use of labour, the hours of work, the standards of employment, the minimum age for employment and other legal requirements affect labour supply (and cost) and again vary geographically.

Finally, in this treatment of geographical variations in labour supply we have to consider the importance of food supplies. No significant level of industrial development would be possible if adequate food supplies to sustain the workers employed in industry were not forthcoming. In most advanced economies the ability to obtain such supplies is now taken for granted. Most normal locations for industrial activity within such countries possess developed connections with areas of food surplus. The movement of foodstuffs within and between countries has reached such a peak of efficiency that, provided the ability to pay is there, there need be little consideration of food supplies in relation to industrial labour supplies. But it was not always so, and it is not invariably the case at the present time. Indeed, for a large proportion of the world's population the provision of simple nutritional needs occupies much, and often the whole, of the productive effort of man. This is particularly the case in south-east Asia. Over large areas there is little or no food surplus above the needs of the agrarian worker to support a significant level of industrial development. Not only does a food surplus allow some transfer of labour to manufacturing and associated occupations, it also provides the agricultural worker with an income with which he may purchase the products of industrial activity. For weighty reasons, therefore, agricultural productivity is always the keystone of prosperity. It was, for example, the increased productivity in agriculture brought about by the agrarian revolution of the eighteenth century that made possible the progressive concentration of labour into manufacturing industries in the United Kingdom. Nowadays in advanced communities little consideration need be given by an entrepreneur to food supplies in making his location decision in the great majority of likely cases. In under-developed countries, however, the supply of labour to industry is still gravely restricted by food supply conditions, and industrial advance will depend primarily upon increased production in agriculture. Viewed internationally, therefore, the location of industry is affected by food supplies, through its effect on the supply of industrial labour. The major concentrations of labour and industry occur in those regions of the world where labour's nutritional requirements are readily satisfied.

The need for special skills is a further factor of importance in influencing and explaining the location of industry. Some industries still call for a high degree of manual skill. Such processes often tend to concentrate at the point where the industry first grew up and this area naturally attracts newcomers in the business. The small metal product trades of Sheffield have already been quoted as an example, but a variety of skills in many differing trades is localised in many centres: London still houses highly skilled workers in the period furniture and ladies' tailoring trades; the craftsmen gunsmiths of Birmingham still ply their individual techniques; the Potteries still contain highly skilled craftsmen making specialised pottery products. Wherever individuality still counts and the product of an individual's specialised skill still commands a market, centres of special labour skills remain. But the range of such products is declining in the machine and automatic age, and the influence of special manual skills in new location decisions is similarly declining. All labour-oriented industries have an incentive to reduce their dependence on labour, which to a greater or smaller degree they tend to accomplish by developing and increasing mechanisation, but this incentive is particularly strong for firms oriented to special labour skills. Less and less of modern manufacturing industry output is dependent on craftsmen's ability as methods of production are perfected that can substitute the machine for the worker's skill.

In considering these points on labour costs, supply and skills we should note that the possession of labour advantages of any sort by an area is usually transitory, being most effective in the short-term situation. In the long term these geographical variations can be modified or even removed by migration of people and skills, by the acquisition of basic skills, by the development of new methods of production, by changing attitudes and so on. We should re-emphasise, too, that labour considerations are becoming of less importance, relative to other considerations, with increasing mechanisation and automation. Thus the labour component in the total cost of an automobile has steadily fallen as more advance techniques have been applied to production. It should be noted, however, that specialised automatic machinery is capable of doing only those operations for which it has been designed. Labour, by contrast, is adaptable and therefore is likely to retain some influence as a locating feature.

We must not leave the impression that the modern industrial worker is becoming entirely an automaton performing routine operations. It is true that, as we have just intimated, the specialised type of craftsman's skill is declining in importance; but there is still a need for much highly skilled labour in mechanised production.

'Mechanisation gives rise to a demand for super-skilled men, both for the maintenance of expensive and intricate plant, and for such occupations as tool making, the importance of which is very greatly increased by mechanisation. Operatives skilled in particular trades are therefore still required, and their availability may have some influence on the location of industries in which they find employment.'[4]

This, although written in 1939, remains true in the age of 'automation'. Further, although the role of 'super skill' may affect a decreasing number of individual employees (while becoming more vital than ever in the operation of industrial processes), many operations call for some skill in a narrow field. A fair proportion of industrial workers may still, therefore, be entitled to the appellation of 'skilled' and most of the remainder will be 'semi-skilled'. We have emphasised that even the simplest of industrial processes requires a certain basic technique and aptitude which is *not* the common possession of labour everywhere. Thus, though labour considerations are becoming of less importance as a major factor in location decisions for a wide range of industry, they remain an important secondary consideration. They will affect, for example, the precise location decision within a generally satisfactory region, or be the deciding factor as between two or more otherwise equally satisfactory locations.

In times of full employment the influence of labour on location decisions is naturally enhanced. During the first ten post-war years, labour was sometimes in desperately short supply in the

United Kingdom and other countries. During this period many enterprises not normally affected strongly by labour requirements were forced to give labour supply priority consideration in seeking locations for new plant. Not only had a suitable location to possess an adequate pool of labour; it also had to be attractive to key personnel. In the United Kingdom such conditions of labour supply influenced many enterprises to consider location in the pre-war depressed areas, where easily trainable labour was available and to which key personnel could be attracted by special induo ments. This influence of labour supply dovetailed neatly with government policy for the location of industry, an aspect that is dealt with in a subsequent chapter.

The availability of capital and related influences

The need for capital also affects the location of industry and the type, and costs, of production in various locations. This may be held as scarcely a field for geographic study, being more appropriate to the economist. But the availability of capital does vary regionally and, more importantly, internationally, while capital itself is also of varying degrees of mobility. Thus capital has some geographical expression which, since it influences the location of economic activity, calls for consideration here. Geographical variations in the price of capital are not necessarily of the same order or even in the same direction as variations in the price of labour. Whichever is the cheaper in any area relative to any other area may therefore be used by skilful management to offset the disadvantage imposed by the dearer element.

Two kinds of capital may be distinguished, capital goods or equipment on the one hand and money capital on the other. The two are closely connected, for the only objective of money capital, in this context, is to procure equipment and working stocks; loans negotiated in money terms are often in fact provided in the form of equipment. But there is a significant difference between the two. Capital equipment in place is relatively immobile, and this is specially true of heavy equipment, which is so important to many industrial processes. Its value lies in its output or as scrap. This is a major reason for geographical inertia: heavy investment in fixed capital is not willingly 'written off' until its useful term of life has been served. Fixed capital is also not without influence on current location decisions. The existence of much capital invest-ment in a geographical area may cause new enterprises to be attracted to that area—either because their processes are associ-

ated in some way with the existing investment, or because they
hope to profit from other external economies arising from such
investment. Further, investment by industrial promotion bodies
in fixed capital assets (especially buildings) is often used as a
device to attract entrepreneurs by the offer of modern plant, immediately available and adequately serviced, sometimes also on
attractive financial terms.

Money capital is, however, much more mobile, though the
precise degree of mobility depends on a variety of considerations.
Money capital is a commodity which, like any other commodity,
has to be bought. The quantity available for any particular use
depends, other things being equal, on the price offered. There are
normally many possible outlets for investment capital and any
proposed use must compete for it at around the prevailing price
(i.e. the rate of interest), having regard to the security of the
investment and the certainty of returns. In advanced economies
'risk capital' is usually quite readily available for the promotion of
new enterprises or the development of promising new internal
areas. Thus the movement of a number of small aircraft manufacturers from the north-east of USA to Texas, Oklahoma and
Kansas is attributed to the readiness of oil financiers there to put
up the necessary money.[5] Within their own national frontiers
investors in most countries feel a certain sense of security, being
assured at least of honest dealing or of remedy at law in default of
that. Thus money capital is usually highly mobile internally. The
Federal Reserve Bank of Boston, for example, makes more than
40 per cent of its loans to borrowers outside of the New England
region. Almost one-half of the total goes to regions west of Ohio.[6]

Money capital is not so mobile across national boundaries, for
official controls are normally imposed and the risks involved are
greater. Much depends on the type of economy, and the attitudes,
prospects and governmental stability of the area of projected investment. Any move that improves the prospects for industrial
development in a country or region will result in increased attention from foreign capital sources. The establishment of the
Common Market of the 'Six' in Europe, for example, is bringing
about a considerable expansion of industrial capacity in the
countries concerned, since it provides, among other things, a
larger 'home market' for industrial enterprise. This is proving
attractive to American and other overseas investors who desire to
participate in industrial and other projects within the Common
Market area.[7]

An important distinction between advanced and under-developed countries is found in the existence on the one hand and the absence on the other of a highly developed money and credit system, providing, for example, institutions for savings, co-operative credit associations, stock markets, industrial development corporations and banking and insurance services. Such organisations enable many capital needs to be met in the form of credit and thus assist in the establishment of industry. For example, the development of certain farm processing industries, such as milk canning, in the south of USA was to some extent dependent upon the ability of farmers to obtain credit from local banks to enable them to develop and expand their output of the required foods. Without confidence in the farmer's ability to obtain and to utilise capital to improve production, the industries processing farm produce would have seen little hope of developing their operations in the south.[8] Again, in the Common Market countries schemes have been introduced to extend banking services and to provide for co-operation between groups of banks. These developments improve the services offered to industrialists and give the co-operating banks ability to lend large quantities of capital for industrial projects on the grand scale.

This sort of provision is not readily available in most under-developed countries. How then can such economies obtain the necessary capital to undertake progressive investment? As in other countries, capital must either be saved out of current income or be borrowed from abroad.[9] If national income is very low and people barely eke out a living, there can be no high level of internal saving, for there is little margin of production over consumption to be set aside for the increase of production in the future. Apart from the adoption of extreme measures of forced saving, as in USSR in the early Five Year Plans, ignoring the inevitable results of misery for many, there is one significant alternative—borrowing from abroad. The absence of such financial institutions as were mentioned above may impede this process but is not an insuperable obstacle. More important is the discouragement of international mobility of capital by the attitudes of the people, and even the governments, of many under-developed areas.[10] Paradoxically, the overseas investor, so essential to economic growth and well-being, is often highly unpopular, the target of much abuse and criticism, if not worse. W. A. Lewis in his *Report on Industrialization and the Gold Coast* (1953) put the issue bluntly: 'Whatever the foreigner's faults may be, the fact remains that the

Gold Coast needs him more than he needs the Gold Coast. . . .
The Gold Coast cannot gain by creating an atmosphere towards
foreign capital which makes foreigners reluctant to invest [there].'[11]
The statement is equally applicable elsewhere.

Only by a freer flow of capital across international boundaries
can the more backward economies hope to improve their condition in reasonably quick time. Much of this essential capital
inflow can, and does, come in the form of foreign government
loans and grants. This particular flow, it may be assumed, is
affected more by political than by economic considerations. It is a
vital element, but is controlled by no consistent economic reasoning. By contrast the private investor distributes his capital for
strictly economic motives. He needs to feel some security in his
investment, an expectation of acceptable returns and freedom
from the fear of governmental instability which might lead even
to the expropriation of his assets without recompense. Unfortunately he can often be given no reliable assurance on these points
and the international mobility of capital is therefore impaired, to
the detriment of all.

Enterprise and management
The efficient application of capital and labour in a modern productive enterprise depends on the general level of business organisation and management in the region concerned. Unless men
competent in the numerous and essential tasks of these higher
levels of labour are available, no economic advance is possible.
This fact justifies a brief treatment of this class of labour separately
from that of other labour. A complex modern industrial economy
demands an adequate supply of men with skills and experience in
technical knowledge, administrative ability, capacity to control
others and marketing 'know-how'. The skilled entrepreneur must
be capable of policy formation and planning, the setting of
objectives and standards, the interpreting of a variety of data,
forecasting, evaluating, supervising, making decisions and so on.
Clearly (though the entrepreneur cannot be a superman!) he provides the dynamism of industrial growth, and poor management
can have serious results.[12]

Established industrial centres usually possess a good supply of
men in the managerial class, and of men receiving the necessary
training and experience in the art of management. This plays a part
in location decisions. In seeking new locations firms naturally
ascertain whether the prospective area has men of executive

ability or, failing that, whether it is, or would become, attractive to such men. In this the physical attractions of the area may be important. In an analysis of post-war industrial migration to Utah and Colorado, Garwood[13] records that climate played an important part in the location decisions of some of the firms concerned. Some maintained that climate was the major consideration, not because of its contribution to production, but because the owners and operators wished to live in the region. Included in this group were furniture manufacturers, mattress makers and the producers of items of stationery. A further comment is made on this in Chapter 7.

Managerial ability is usually fairly mobile, especially within national boundaries, and an area with good prospects can usually attract men of ability. The attraction is naturally augmented if the location is also a physically desirable one. But 'imported' managerial and executive personnel are not always sufficient. Local participation in management may be immediately desirable and in the long run essential. Men with potential ability may well be available in most probable locations in an advanced economy, and a short period of training would bring them to the point where they could be useful in minor executive posts while gaining the experience for advanced managerial positions.

Both of these features, mobility and relatively quickly developed local ability, are relevant to the situation in less developed countries. Here one of the greatest obstacles to industrial development is the general lack of trained and experienced men of high executive and managerial ability. The development of these skills in such an economy cannot be an overnight affair for, unless schooled by practical experience, even first-rate managerial material can do much harm to a productive enterprise. If native management is, then, not available in sufficient quantities, the only alternative is to attempt to import it. The mobility of managerial and entrepreneurial skill across international borders is somewhat similar to that of capital. The rates offered must be competitive and have regard to the fact that the individual executive may have to be lured from a developed area, with its many attractions and amenities. Some sacrifice is being called for, and this usually has to be recompensed by higher financial rewards. Unfortunately, foreign management, like foreign capital, is often regarded with suspicion, distrust and dislike. A hostile attitude is not conducive to the essential mobility of higher executive skills, and failure to attract these higher forms of labour is a serious impediment to industrial growth.

Even a richly endowed country needs these organisational and executive skills if it is to develop a manufacturing economy, for poor management fails to capitalise on good resources. The need for first-class ability is even greater where resources are scarce, for here skill, ingenuity and innovation must offset the lack of a good resource base. Poor management puts a region with material deficiencies into an impossible position commercially. Protection against foreign competition may allow inefficiently managed enterprises to survive, but at a significant cost to the community as a whole. The essence of good management is to capitalise on favourable natural and human resources and to offset adverse environmental features.

[1] For our purposes cost of land will be regarded as a part of capital costs

[2] 'Labour Mobility and Regional Growth', *Economic Geography*, October 1955

[3] See G. L. Reid and D. J. Robertson, *Fringe Benefits, Labour Cost and Social Security*, 1965

[4] 'The Location of Industry in Great Britain', *Political and Economic Planning*, 1939, p. 66

[5] McLaughlin and Robock, op. cit., p. 96

[6] Federal Reserve Bank of Boston, *New England Business Review*, July 1959

[7] See, for example, S. Wellisz, 'The European Common Market and American Trade and Investment', *Journal of Business*, July 1959

[8] McLaughlin and Robock, op. cit., pp. 96–7

[9] In the short term 'deficit financing' may supply some necessary monetary resources. This involves the printing of money, the government getting the first spending. Its effect is inflationary and it is a device that must be used with care

[10] Such attitudes are not unknown elsewhere. A suspicion of the motives of foreign investors often exists even in advanced industrial areas and can act to frustrate the international mobility of capital.

[11] P. 9

[12] For example, the speed and the extent of the contraction of the New England cotton textile industry is attributed by some observers to the poor quality of its management at a critical stage in its history, between the wars. Similar views are held in respect of experiences in certain British industries

[13] *Economic Geography*, January 1953

5

GEOGRAPHICAL CONCENTRATION AND
TECHNOLOGICAL CHANGE

The influences discussed so far have a vital part to play in most location decisions, but we should still be unable satisfactorily to explain existing locations, or their continuing attraction to new enterprises, in those terms alone. The further significant considerations guiding location decisions include the economies a firm may gain by a location in a major centre of industrial production, and sometimes, too, by close geographical association with other productive units in the same industry. On the other hand some firms and industries seek economies of various kinds by dispersing their productive activities. Some existing locations may owe their survival to geographical inertia, while others may owe their rise to advances in technology, and in these circumstances industrial research is a vital influence. This chapter is concerned with all these matters.

Concentration and dispersal: locational effects
One may readily observe from an economic atlas that by far the greatest proportion of total world output of manufactured goods occurs in a few highly concentrated regions or belts of industrial production. It is pertinent to ask why. Many industrial processes have evidently been attracted to the same location, and the process tends to be cumulative. The initial attraction to industry, for example, may have been the availability of energy supplies or the existence of a raw material or a nodal situation, as at a major port or junction of routes. Whatever the reason for the initial establishment of industrial enterprise, the very existence of active industry

may make the location attractive to other industries. Some may want to use the product of an established firm as their material. Thus many steel users are attracted to steel-making centres. Others may want to use a by-product of those industries which may previously have been largely wasted and is therefore available at a cheap rate. For example, waste sulphur recovered from gas scrubbers at gas and coking plant has been used for fertiliser manufacture, and firms using this material will wish to locate close to the gas or coking station. Conversely, new industries may be set up to supply established firms with certain parts, for example with machinery or containers.

As the nucleus grows, it becomes a centre of concentrated earning power, and therefore of purchasing power. In other words it becomes a better and better market for the consumer goods industries, many of which will be attracted to a location in or near this growing centre. The tertiary (service) occupations will also be expanding. The labour supply grows, both in numbers and in its range of industrial skills, still further enhancing the attractions of the location for yet other processes. The initial industrial development may well have called mainly for one broad type of labour, but once this labour is present it follows that other forms of labour could be available. In a location where the leading early industries were those heavy processes that tend to employ a high proportion of males, there would possibly be a pool of unemployed or underemployed women and girls. Lighter industries, especially those employing mainly female labour, might find such a location attractive.

As the centre of industrial activity expands from its initial nucleus, it provides opportunities for achieving certain economies through the geographical concentration of activity. Some of these are further extensions of the attractions just described. Just as a single industry can, up to a point, achieve internal economies as it expands its output and capacity, so the whole mass of industries in a large industrial area can achieve certain important external economies of scale as the industrial capacity of the area grows.

The first of these external economies derives from the principle mentioned above, that a firm may buy in more of its requirements. By this means individual firms can 'contract out' of making (probably on a smaller and comparatively expensive scale) certain necessary parts. These they purchase from another firm which specialises in the production of those parts. Such a specialised firm, with its larger scale of production, can use specialised machinery and reduce its overhead costs. It may also gain in other ways, for example from economies in bulk purchasing of materials. The firms that are buying-in the parts can therefore expect to acquire them more cheaply than by making them themselves, and the whole of their capital, accommodation and labour will be available for the processes they perform themselves. This process of drawing upon a large number of sub-contractors is well exemplified by many important modern industries and affects their location. In the manufacture of aircraft engines and propellors in USA, for instance, it is largely this feature that keeps most capacity in the industry in the north-east, while airframe production and final assembly has, for different reasons, been attracted elsewhere.

In a large and growing industrial centre there is also development and expansion of many essential or useful services. For example, special banking and insurance facilities become available; capital (especially short-term capital) is more readily available and the banks become familiar with the special financial needs of the main industries. Trade journals are produced, providing useful information, both general and specialised. Repair and maintenance services for machinery are also more readily available to firms in a large industrial centre. The speed and cheapness of such services are of great value to the smaller firms that cannot maintain their own servicing staff; but large firms also may save themselves the costs of supporting their own servicing staff when expert outside help is quickly available.

Small-scale and specialised industries also gain great economies by concentrating their activities in a distinctive 'quarter' of a large industrial centre. They can, for example, buy and sell through local middlemen who specialise in their requirements. They can also save considerably by subdivision of the process, which is aided by the physical proximity of the various small units to each other. Investment in plant and floor space can sometimes be cut by the practice of 'putting out' work for workers to do in their own homes. Further, dealers in the product know such specialised centres of production and 'shop around' for their purchases in the area of major concentration. The jewellery and gun quarters in Birmingham and the clothing and furniture-making quarters of East London are distinctive centres of such specialisation of small-scale manufacture.[1]

The large industrial region normally also possesses research organisations whose assistance can be called upon. It may be worth noting here that vigorous research activity is one important means by which an industrial region whose original basis for development has disappeared or declined may maintain its attraction. This will be referred to again below. Transport services will also be adapted to serve the needs of the industries in an area of major industrial concentration, and firms may obtain special rates because of the large volume of traffic provided. Educational services may be oriented towards the requirements of the main industries of the region, especially in technical colleges and evening institutions. The prestige and advertising advantages of a location in the large, well-established centre with a high reputation is a further attraction to industry.

The labour supply in a large industrial centre is also generally adequate and flexible. This allows expansion and reduction of staff to take place with less difficulty than in a small community. The large urban area is itself attractive to labour in many ways. Not only is there a wider choice of employment but there is also the attraction of the educational, cultural, entertainment and other facilities of the big centre. Thus there is usually a steady influx of newcomers to swell the labour force.

There is, however, another side to the picture. At some stage maximum economies of scale will have been achieved and further expansion may result in dis-economies which offset or more than offset the economies. Just when this stage has been reached is not easy to decide in practice, but this is one of the reasons why some industries prefer to disperse their productive capacity. Among the dis-economies or disadvantages of concentration we may mention the following. First, competition between various industries may bid up the prices of materials and factors of production, i.e. labour of all kinds, land and perhaps capital. Secondly, labour in regions of heavy industrial concentration is usually strongly unionised, and militant union activity may affect labour attitudes as well as wages. Strikes may be more common and their effects more widespread, since firms not involved in a dispute may still have their productive processes interrupted or may lose their own labour in a 'sympathy' strike. Further, strikes in the public services will have more severe effects in areas with large industrial concentrations. Thirdly, when a region has grown above a certain size, the provision of services and amenities becomes more costly and taxes must be increased to pay for them. Congestion increases on existing facilities, especially transport, but probably also on things like water supply and waste disposal services, and costs are thereby increased yet further.

Such disadvantages cause some firms to seek a location elsewhere. Sometimes this may mean no more than a move to the
suburbs, where the firm is still within reach of many of the economies of concentration. For other firms, however, an entirely new
location may be sought, often by the opening of branch factories.
Some firms try to avoid having a large proportion of their
capacity in the larger industrial centres, since they achieve certain
advantages from the disperal of their operations. Naturally this
depends upon the type of industry and its locational requirements.
Thus many industries with widely spread markets have found it
advantageous to operate in relatively small and highly dispersed
units. In large countries, as population spread to new areas,
market-oriented industries have an incentive to follow with new
capacity rather than serve the growing area from the older centres
of production. This incentive is increased by the tendency for the
gap between freight rates on raw materials and on finished
products to widen in favour of materials. Similarly, industries
which draw their materials from widely dispersed sources (especially some food-processing plants using agricultural produce) also
tend to be dispersed.

In looking for locations away from the major centres of
industrial activity, firms naturally vary widely in their requirements. Some look for towns with little or no existing industry,
hoping thereby to gain, as we have seen, from the lack of competition for labour and from a favourable attitude on the part of the
community. Others look for a town that already has some
industrial potential, hoping to find suitable labour and possible
sources of supply for component parts or services. In federal
countries state laws also play some part in the dispersal of
industrial capacity. Firms may wish to avoid having all their
capacity in one state to insure against the possibility of adverse
changes in the state law.

An example of the search for economies from dispersal is provided by the electrical products industry in the USA. Two companies dominate the industry, with their home plants in Pittsburgh
and Schenectady. A feature of their present location policy is to
'develop new products at their home plant, but manufacture them
elsewhere, frequently in smaller centres affording lower taxes,
cheaper sites, lower labour costs, lower power costs, or a combination of these advantages'.[2]

In general, however, the economies of concentration are very
real and a wide range of industry continues to be attracted to

established centres of production. Above a certain size these highly significant economies may be partially, or even completely, offset by dis-economies, but little is known about the stage at which this begins to affect significantly the existing industrial structure. At some time or other most of the world's greatest industrial complexes have been thought to be beyond the point where economies are offset by the extra costs incurred in various ways, but industry continues to expand in these centres, showing that many industrialists themselves still think that the major concentration retains numerous advantages.

The geographical association of industries

We noted briefly above the significance of the economies to be achieved by the association of groups of interrelated industries in one location. These can be vital to small-scale enterprises, but are of great value also to establishments of large scale and thus merit some further comment here. The juxtaposition of separate undertakings, pursuing the same kind of process or participating in a sequence of operations, is a common feature of industrial distribution. Such geographically associated establishments participate in those general economies of concentration that have just been discussed. Here, however, we wish to give special emphasis to those economies achieved in a series of related industrial processes by the grouping together in space of a number of separate plants each specialising in a limited contribution to the final product(s) of the area. The features contributing to the economies achieved through this type of locational grouping include the economy of division of labour, obtained by the specialisation of the individual firm on one particular link in the chain of production. This permits the adoption of specialised techniques and machinery that would probably be uneconomic in an individual plant attempting to pursue the whole sequence within its own walls. Moreover, such 'linked' or related industries often require similar types of labour skills and there is room therefore for a relatively high degree of labour mobility between firms.

A further advantage is the easy interchange of materials and products between the linked establishments that is facilitated by geographical proximity. The road is the conveyor belt and the associated establishments probably experience little greater difficulty in moving goods about than a very large-scale enterprise experiences in moving its goods inside its own works. As Sargant Florence puts it, unless the large-scale plant can use special techniques of internal movement (as for example a conveyor belt system) 'crawling' from one adjacent plant to another may be just as cheap as movement within a larger factory.[3]

Where linked industries operate in juxtaposition, there are also available to all participants in the chain certain specialised and general services which afford a considerable economy in the maintenance and servicing staff of individual firms. It is also typical of such industrial environments that some small firms will specialise on processes rather than on products. These can undertake a variety of special work 'put out' by other firms, and are very flexible in operation, able to change the materials that they use, or the shapes they make according to requirements. The existence of such firms is of great value to the type of geographical agglomeration of industries to which we are referring. Finally, as might be expected, a close relationship, almost a partnership, grows up among related firms in a given geographical area. The ability, for example, of members of the group to meet without inconvenience to discuss common problems and matters of mutual interest is a not inconsiderable advantage of close geographical association.

We may broadly distinguish four common types of linkage. The first is a vertical linkage, the interrelationship of separate firms each normally forming one stage in a series of operations. In the non-ferrous metal trades, for example, the sequence is from the refining stage to the shaping of the metal, to the further processing of the rough shapes, to the manufacture and, finally, to the finishing of the particular end product.

A second type of linkage is horizontal or lateral. Here separate firms produce the many individual parts and accessories that come together at some later stage to be assembled into a finished product. There is a horizontal linkage, for example, among the separate plants making the many individual parts that will finally be assembled into a motor bicycle.

A third form of association is diagonal, where a firm makes a product, or provides a service, that is required at various stages in the vertical process. Its contacts are thus with a number of separate plants and it does not form a link in a given chain of processes in the same way as the horizontally or vertically related firms. Firms providing tools for other plants in their area, for instance, or specialising in a process which is available to any firm in the district (e.g. stamping or piercing), are said to link diagonally with the other plants.

A fourth kind of linkage is based on what may be termed 'common roots'. It may be best explained in the words of a survey of the Birmingham and Black Country region carried out by the West Midland Group,[4] which refers to the linkage of 'industries using in common or diverging from certain processes, services or skills, provided locally and not elsewhere to any extent. In the conurbation several industries diverge from the secondary metal-working processes and are thus laterally related to one another. Most of them depend not only on common processes but on a common pool of labour specially skilled.' The survey goes on to cite the making of guns and locks as examples of industries mutually dependent on the metal-working processes and pools of skilled labour in the conurbation.

So important may be the economies to be gained by the geographical association of establishments linked in the ways described that new entrants to the industry may have little choice in their location. To begin operations on a site in or near the established centre may well be a pre-condition of success. A location elsewhere would bring an inability to share fully the economies available to the relatively tightly knit group. In addition the 'social' relationships among the linked firms in the main centre, which commonly create a feeling of loyalty to the group, may well make it difficult for a newcomer in a location away from the recognised geographical area to obtain regular and reliable orders.

The geographical association of linked industries is thus a highly important feature of industrial distributions. It is well exemplified in the multitudinous trades of the west Midland region,[5] but is common to all really large centres. By such physical proximity each participant in the chain benefits not only from the advantages the location itself possesses, but also from the considerable external economies of concentration. Nationally, such considerations may lead to the concentration of most of the capacity in a given industry in a few large centres of production. It must be remembered, however, that in these, as in other instances, the places where these concentrations develop and the degree of concentration in them will depend on the nature of the products, the labour supply, the size, type and location of markets—in short on all those influences we have discussed in previous chapters. Linkage, that is to say, is a derived, not an original, advantage; it is a method of utilising and increasing the advantages of an already developed area.

Geographical inertia

We have many times referred to the necessity for looking into the past to find a rational explanation of present industrial distributions. Often the survival of an old established industrial area rests on geographical inertia. This is a 'built-in' resistance to decline and it is sometimes extremely strong in preserving the location of industry. For various reasons—a raw material supply, a power supply, a nodal location for existing transport services and so on —an area may have become an important centre of industrial production. The factors that initially caused industry to settle at this point may decline in their importance, or even disappear, but the industrial centre often remains. Not all locations losing their original *raison d'être*, however, continue to flourish as industrial centres. The small water power sites of England and western Europe are often littered with the relics of small-scale industry. But areas where development has been on a large scale are very likely to continue their industrial activity, even after their original locational advantages have disappeared.

The reasons for this may be classified broadly into two groups. First, there is the fact that capital equipment (plant and machinery) is highly immobile and often possessed of a long life. This represents a heavy investment, which is not readily written off. Owners of such expensive capital usually strive to keep it in operation even in the face of severe competition. A further considerable factor is that it is often much cheaper to expand industrial capacity at an existing site than to construct a new plant on a new site. It has been estimated, for example, that to construct a new steel plant on a new site costs about three times as much as adding the same capacity to an existing plant. The additional costs would be even greater in buliding on a new site in an entirely new location, for here both construction costs and operating costs are likely, at least initially, to be greater than in a location near an established centre of production. There are, of course, many other issues in this type of decision, as for example the changing location of markets, but the savings to be made by expanding on existing sites, or in an existing industrial area, are of great significance in a location decision.

These considerations are reinforced by the operation of the second group of forces making for geographical inertia. This, briefly, is that other advantages grow up in a developed area and these may offset the loss of the original attraction. Among these

D

added advantages are the growth of a skilled labour force, the development of transport facilities to suit the area, the extablishment of a reputation, the presence of facilities of all kinds, economic and social, in existing centres of industry and the emergence of linkage in industry. Many of the features (described above) of large industrial concentrations make for geographical inertia, while we have already noted (Chapter 2) that the existing structure of freight rates may often favour the old established region.

There is therefore strong resistance to the abandonment of an established industrial area from all the vested interests concerned, including capital investments, jobs held, skills attained, social capital and all the impedimenta of industrial life and work. Moreover, a large centre of industry will have accumulated many other market-oriented and service industries. It has therefore been cogently argued that the ability of a centre of manufacturing to keep an industry greatly exceeds its original ability to attract it. Geographical inertia is clearly at its strongest in areas of heavy industry. Major examples of inertia are provided by the existing location of much steel-making capacity at and near Pittsburgh in the United States and at Sheffield in the United Kingdom. In both cases the original location attractions have declined in their importance or relevance, but the legacies of the past plus the advantages of the proximity of many large steel-using industries combine to ensure that these centres remain highly important in the steel-producing business of their countries. In a different case, it is largely inertia that keeps some 40 per cent of USA textile machinery manufacturing employment in New England (in 1962) although most of the textile mills are now located elsewhere.

Technological change

The importance of technological advance has been touched upon in discussing raw materials, fuel and power, transport and other influences on industrial location. Our short historical retrospects have in reality been largely a discussion of the influence of technological developments. At this point, however, we may conveniently summarise these influences, which are clearly of great importance in the location of industrial activity.

In some cases technological advance has brought about an increased concentration of industrial activity at certain favoured locations. Thus, the development of power-driven machinery in the textile industry had the effect of encouraging the growth of marked geographical concentrations in the industry, replacing the more dispersed patterns of the domestic system. In other cases technological advance has released an industry from a highly restricted locational pattern and permitted, or encouraged, a wider choice of possible locations. Thus, while metallurgical coke could be obtained only by the wasteful beehive process, the coking industry in the United States was strongly oriented to coking coal in order to save unnecessary weight in the transported material. With the development of the by-product ovens and improvements in steel-making practices, however, it became possible and desir able to extract the by-products from the gases previously wasted and to use the remaining gases for heating in the iron and steel plant. At the same time a lower grade of bituminous coal could also be used to produce metallurgical coke from by-product ovens. Consequently the location of the coking industry shifted from the coking-coal field to the centres where the by-products could be utilised, i.e. at the iron and steel centres themselves. The economies achieved by the use of the gases outweighed the extra transport costs of moving raw coal. Thus Connellsville, which had dominated the production of metallurgical coke in the United States before the first world war, rapidly declined in importance, and the coking industry is now much more dispersed, largely coinciding with the iron and steel locations.

The development of substitutes may also affect industrial location. This effect is illustrated by the recent development of substitute raw materials in ammonia production. Before 1939 coal and coke formed the material basis of over 90 per cent of world output of ammonia. The economical supply of these materials had consequently determined the major locations of the industry. Many countries with a large demand for ammonia had little choice but to import it. Technological developments since 1939, however, have made it possible to utilise natural gas, fuel oil and refinery gases in ammonia synthesis. Now only about 40 per cent of world ammonia is derived from coal and coke, and the industry is far more widely distributed.[6] It follows that industries based on ammonia (nitrogen production, for example) are also more widespread.

The locational effects of progressive advances in power production and utilisation, in transport facilities, in techniques of mineral exploitation and utilisation and so on are of great importance, and some results of such developments have been indicated in earlier sections. Further, techniques of production that place less of a premium on skilled labour are constantly

being developed, and this, as we have noted, is a process that progressively frees industry from locations where specific skills exist.
We should remember, however, that although new developments
may make a new location possible, or even desirable, geographical
inertia may slow down or even prevent the rise of new centres.

The importance of research

At this stage the place of research in advanced economies may be
mentioned, since virtually all technological progress now comes
from research specifically carried on for that purpose. In this
contest we should distinguish between fundamental research, for
example in chemistry or physics, which is concerned with acquir-
ing an understanding of how the natural forces act and interact,
and industrial research, which is aimed at finding out how to apply
the results obtained by fundamental research to new or more
efficient production. In practice the dividing line is not always
clear. Most modern industries and even many individual large
firms now maintain large research laboratories, whose primary
function is to investigate the problems of the industry or the firm;
but often the scientific staffs of these research organisations en-
gage in pieces of fundamental research in connection with or in
addition to their more obviously practical investigations. The
electronics industry, the complex plastics industry and a wide
range of chemical industries are examples of entirely new industries
created in modern times by the success of industrial research teams
in translating new discoveries from laboratory to factory scale.

Research and innovation are of vital importance in a mature
industrial region, i.e. a region in which the early stages of industrial development are long past and in which the old industries
have declined in the face of competition from more recently
industrialised areas. Old England and New England are perhaps
the best examples of such mature industrial regions, and both
have had to face serious decline in their old staple industries,
especially textiles. Both have been turning more and more to
advanced engineering industries, in which they keep ahead by
labour skill and continued technological advance. They both
illustrate the necessity of progressive adoption of new products,
or new ways of producing and improving on old products. This
process depends directly upon research, and research institutions
are a vital part of the economic structure of mature industrial
regions.[7] To the extent that they are successful they constitute an
important element contributing to geographical inertia.

Although research and development work is vital to the sustained health of an industrial economy, relevant statistics are not easily come by. For the UK a Department of Scientific and Industrial Research report in 1958 remains the chief source. This showed that in 1955 about £300 million were spent on research and development in British industries, about £183 million of this being spent in the private industrial sector.[8] The distribution of the latter sum and of employment in research over the main industrial groups is shown in Table 6. An interesting feature is the prominu-

TABLE 6

DISTRIBUTION OF EMPLOYMENT AND EXPENDITURE
IN RESEARCH AND DEVELOPMENT
BY PRIVATE MANUFACTURING INDUSTRY,
UK 1955

Industry	*Employment* %	*Expenditure* %
Aircraft	27·5	43·7
Electrical engineering and electrical goods	23·4	18·2
Chemicals and allied trades	16·4	12·8
Non-electrical engineering and ship-building	10·7	8·4
Vehicles and components (excl. aircraft)	5·6	4·3
Textiles	3·5	2·7
Metal manufacture	3·4	2·6
	90·5	92·7
Absolute totals	109,500	£183 million

Source: DSIR, Estimates of Resources Devoted to Scientific and Engineering Research, p. 10

ence in research activity of the first three industrial groups, all of them to a greater or lesser extent 'new' industries. This of itself suggests that a high level of industrial research is helping to maintain the United Kingdom as a favourable location for the establishment and growth of new processes and products.

The location of research facilities is also of great significance. Not only is industrial research a large industry in its own right, but a location where research facilities are available is often attractive to firms that wish to use the products of research or to participate in it. The DSIR study (see Table 7) shows that there is an important concentration of research employment in private industry in the southern part of the UK—about 55 per cent in the area south of a line from the Wash to Gloucester, an area which contains about one-third of the total industrial labour force in the United Kingdom. North of this line only the Midland and the

TABLE 7

REGIONAL DISTRIBUTION OF RESEARCH AND DEVELOPMENT
WORKERS IN PRIVATE MANUFACTURING INDUSTRY,
UK 1955

Region	Employment in research and development work %	Total industrial labour force %	Total population %
Great Britain	*100*	*100*	*100*
London and South-east	28·8	19·9	22·1
Eastern	9·5	5·1	6·7
Southern	7·1	3·9	5·7
South-western	9·1	4·1	6·2
Midlands	13·1	14·2	9·1
North Midlands	5·9	7·6	7·0
Yorkshire (East and West Ridings)	5·3	10·1	8·3
North-western	13·8	17·2	13·0
Northern	3·1	5·2	6·4
Scottish	2·7	9·1	10·4
Welsh	1·7	3·6	5·3

Source: DSIR, Estimates of Resources Devoted to Scientific and Engineering Research, p. 19

north-western regions have a significant share, the rest of the United Kingdom (which contains *c.* 35 per cent of the industrial labour force) having under 19 per cent of total research and development workers in private industry. Scotland especially seems poorly served.

The vitality of the London and Birmingham conurbations is illustrated in the high proportion of total industrial research that takes place in their regions. The London and south-east and the

Midlands regions together have *c.* 42 per cent of total research and development workers in private industrial establishments in the United Kingdom. This reflects, and is reflected in, the dominating position held by these two industrial regions in the economy. The table excludes workers in grant-aided Research Associations and in DSIR stations, but these are again mainly found in the London region.

'One of the main reasons for the apparent concentration of research and development in the south is the location of most of the aircraft industry, the radio industry and the newer developments of electrical engineering in southern England. Another contributory reason is that some of the largest manufacturing companies with head offices in London have in recent years established separate research laboratories in country districts in southern England although their manufacturing interests may be more widely scattered.'[9]

Generally, therefore, it may be held that the southern regions of the country, and especially the London conurbation and neighbouring areas, possess many attractions to industrialists who wish to establish a research plant. Nearness to London permits research institutions to have close contact with the departments of state that are responsible for awarding valuable government research contracts. The area provides attractive opportunities and a variety of prospects for highly qualified research personnel, while the wide range of academic, library and other facilities and proximity to other research stations are important additional attractions. Such a large centre is also one where a new invention may be most readily tested and applied, and where a large market containing potential customers exists. In a broader way this concentration of research activity is in itself a further stimulus to general industrial activity in this part of the country, and to the concentration there of the modern, research based, industries. The UK experience has parallels elsewhere. The great concentrations of the electronic product and missile industries in the USA, for example, are in close proximity to the major centres of research, which command government contracts of enormous value.[10]

[1] See J. M. Wise, 'On the Evolution of the Jewellery and Gun Quarters of Birmingham', *Transactions of the Institute of British Geographers*, 1949; J. E. Martin, 'Three Elements in the Industrial Geography of Greater London in J. T. Coppock and H. C. Prince (Eds), *Greater London*, 1964

[2] G. Alexandersson, *The Industrial Structure of American Cities*, 1956, p. 49

[3] P. Sargant Florence, *Investment, Location and Size of Plant*, 1948, p. 53

⁴ The West Midland Group, *Conurbation. A Survey of Birmingham and the Black Country*, 1948, p. 132

⁵ See, for example, *Birmingham and its Regional Setting*, ed. M. J. Wise, British Association, 1950; and the West Midland Group, op. cit.

⁶ See the *Economist*, 23 May 1959

⁷ An analysis of this process in the New England context is made by R. C. Estall, *New England. A Study in Industrial Adjustment.*

⁸ Department of Scientific and Industrial Research, *Estimates of Resources Devoted to Scientific and Engineering Research and Development in British Manufacturing Industry, 1955*, 1958. The remaining £117 million was spent by the government on work relating to defence, the nationalised industries, etc. Over two-thirds of the expenditure in the private sector, however, also came from government sources and this tends to be concentrated in the aircraft industry, thus helping it to dominate the table of expenditure

⁹ Ibid., p. 20

¹⁰ See R. C. Estall, op cit., chapters 4 and 7.

6

THE EFFECTS OF GOVERNMENT ACTIVITY

Although of fundamental importance the influences already discussed are not the only ones that affect the location of manufacturing activity. Some of the other influences are external to the actual productive process whose location they affect, but they can, and do, influence the final choice between alternative locations and may even cause manufacturing industry to be undertaken in otherwise less suitable locations. The most important of these external influences are the activities of central governments, to which we shall address ourselves in this chapter.

Government action affecting the location of industry is not confined to totalitarian countries but is prevalent in all economies today. The methods may be more direct in totalitarian states, but the more refined influences at work in democracies can still be extremely effective in moulding the geographical patterns of industrial production. This intervention by governments in the location of manufacturing activity may be incidental or deliberate. It may, for example, arise unintended from legislation intended primarily to achieve other aims; or it may be deliberate intervention in location decisions for any one or more of a number of reasons. Further, this governmental influence can be either positive or negative in nature: on the one hand it may encourage new industrial growth or developments; on the other it may inhibit them. Thus a given industrial enterprise may owe its location partly to governmental influences, either positively, because original advantages were augmented by government activity, or negatively, because an otherwise more attractive location had to be passed over.

Governments affect industrial activity generally through many normal laws, as for example those relating to hours of work, minimum wages, safety and health requirements, minimum ages of working force, legal requirements in organisation and so on. Such legislation will affect industrial location only where there are geographical variations in its application. In a country such as the United Kingdom, with its unitary form of government, this type of legislation is universally applicable. From the point of view of employing young labour, for example, it does not matter whether one is in Bristol or Newcastle—the law is the same. In federal systems, however, variations do occur, as, for example, in the various states of the Union in the United States. Differences from one state to another in legal requirements therefore play some part in location decisions. In New England, for example, it was illegal, until comparatively recently, to employ women after 6 pm, while in the southern states they could be employed on night shifts. The less restrictive laws in the south constituted a strong attraction to some firms, especially in the cotton textile industry.

General industrial activity, and location decisions, can also be affected by government taxation and expenditure. The effects of differential taxation are likely to be greater under a federal system of government, where State variations exist, than under a unitary system. Taxes do not, however, generally form a highly significant percentage of total costs, and their effects can be over-stressed. They may serve to tilt the location decision as between two otherwise equally attractive areas, causing entrepreneurs to steer away from areas that have a reputation for high taxation. This may be unfair in many instances, and even short-sighted. A state with a somewhat higher level of taxation may well be one in which the quality of the services provided (from which the industrialist directly or indirectly benefits) is superior to that of low tax areas. Nevertheless the fact remains that some firms avoid reputedly high tax states, one of the best examples in the USA being Massachusetts, where local taxes are especially heavy. The real position in Massachusetts may not be as bad as the reputation; and indeed the tax structure here is in some respects more favourable to industry than that in competing areas,[1] but the reputation remains and continues to affect the view taken of the attractiveness of this state to industry.

Sometimes geographical variations of taxation in federal countries are not due entirely to the individual member states. Taxes imposed by the federal government may also vary regionally, being designed specifically to encourage developments in certain regions. In Australia, for example, a zone allowance attempts to increase the incentive to establish enterprises in the more remote and difficult parts of the continent. Thus a large area of northern Australia qualifies for maximum allowance—but the scale of such relief seems relatively small, with little effect on industry. The principle, however, is worthy of note.

Taxes may also operate differentially against an individual industry, especially perhaps taxes on the product. Purchase tax is an example. Demand for the product of the industry concerned is artificially lowered by the application of a tax, normally on a percentage basis, which is reflected in the retail price. This can bring about a reduction of activity in the manufacture of the product concerned and may stimulate the production and sale of substitutes. Such government activity affects the general industrial situation, but has little effect upon the internal location of industry. As between different countries, however, the picture formed of relative tax burdens will affect the attractiveness of particular countries to investors, especially foreign investors, and thus affect their prospects of general industrial growth. A discriminatory tax, for example, will discourage the affected industry and will restrict its essential home market. Consequently its ability to adopt productive methods from which the greatest economies of scale can be obtained is reduced. This will affect its competitive position relative to other producing countries, lead to a declining export market and even possibly to an under-cutting in the home market. Internationally, therefore, the location of industry can be affected by the general taxation policies of governments.

The role of government, however, is not confined to relieving people and firms of their money. Governments are also the biggest spenders in most economies. Where this money is spent and what it is spent on can be a vital consideration in the economies of areas within a country, and even of overseas areas in the case of intergovernmental loans and grants. Here we are not speaking of that part of the government's programme that is specifically for the promotion of industry. General government expenditure can stimulate new growth or bolster up old units and areas. By raising incomes in the regions where money is spent, governments stimulate the demand for goods and services and thus the industries supplying them. This vast expenditure need follow no set rules. It is based not only on economic criteria but also on political, strategic, or social considerations. It can, therefore, change the type of geographical distribution of incomes that would result from a free play of economic forces, and changes in the distribution of income means changes in the distribution of markets. Tax money raised in one area and spent in another has the effect of reducing incomes in the area of origin and raising incomes in the area of spending. Developments in Arizona may be quoted as an example. Here, both population and personal incomes have grown rapidly since the early 1940's. But these advances owe much to a high level of Federal Government spending in the state, especially on military and associated requirements. A large proportion of the income of this state is still derived from federal expenditures, which are thus very important in stimulating economic development there. Other states (Alaska, California and Washington, for example) also owe a great deal to the high level of Federal Government expenditure in their territories.

Apart from the effects of general government activity, industrial location is also, and more particularly, affected by both direct and indirect government intervention. The reasons for such intervention are many, but may be summed up as follows:

1. the desire to assist national industries against foreign competition;

2. the desire to develop strategically important industries;

3. the desire to have strategically important industries safely located;

4. the desire to avoid heavy and continuous unemployment;

5. the desire to diversify the industrial structure of regions over-dependent on a limited range of industries;

6. the desire to limit industrial growth in large conurbations.

Indirect governmental influence on location

Among the tools that governments use to foster industrial growth, or to preserve it, are the erection of tariff barriers, the application of quota systems to restrict imports, the negotiation of restrictive trade agreements and financial manipulations of various kinds. These have the universal result of restricting competition from overseas and permitting activity in lines that might not survive free competition. Industrialists often exert strong pressure on governments to impose, maintain or increase such barriers to competition. Internal price support schemes also exist to help producers of certain goods. We are not here concerned to assess the rightness or wrongness of such activity, but merely to indicate its effects on the location of economic activity. It is clear that these activities affect the general world distribution of industry. Countries will be found to possess productive enterprises in fields in which they possess little cost advantage. The original decision on the precise location of such an enterprise may well be difficult to analyse satisfactorily. Normally one would assume that a point is chosen where the productive cost disadvantages are least. Once established, however, the location may well become its own *raison d'être* and, if associated industries are progressively developed near by, may eventually improve its cost position *vis à-vis* foreign competitors.

Industrial activity and location are also affected by a government's unemployment policies. These normally aim at establishing an adequate minimum of spending power and at increasing labour mobility between jobs and between areas. For the latter purpose Labour Exchanges have been set up in some countries to bring vacancies to the notice of the unemployed labour; training schemes are sometimes developed to promote greater mobility between jobs of different types. Regional mobility can be assisted by financial grants, by the provision of accommodation in the receiving areas and in other ways. By such methods the United Kingdom government attempted to ease the effects of the great inter-war depression. By the payment of unemployment benefits the personal incomes of people in affected areas do not fall below a set minimum, and this naturally affects beneficially the retail sale situation and the fortunes of local firms providing consumer goods and services.

Governments can also indirectly influence the location of industry by their control of land use. In the United Kingdom, for example, there is a comprehensive control of all forms of land use. This acts mainly in a negative way, prohibiting industrial development at certain points. While industrialists can be told where no development will be permitted, there is no compulsory power to direct them to approved sites in areas 'zoned' for industrial development. Nevertheless the comprehensive control of land use is an important way of influencing industrial location, and is at its most effective in times of boom and inflation, when industry is seeking to expand.

Direct government influence on location
Strategic, economic and social requirements have caused governments to intervene directly in the location of industrial activity. Thus, in order to ensure that important war capacity is available

in relevant industries, and to achieve the greatest possible safety in location, governments have influenced investment in, and the location of, such industries. This is perhaps especially true of the iron and steel industry. The iron and steel plant based on the Salzgitter-Wattenstedt iron ores, near Hanover in Germany, was the direct result of the Nazi government's interest in their development. The purpose was to develop iron and steel capacity based on home ores at a point well removed from international frontiers. The Geneva steel plant in Utah, Colorado, is the result of the wartime activity of the Federal Government in the USA. No private firm would have considered putting an iron and steel works in this location without government assistance.

Munition and other war factories have also been regularly located with an eye to safety or to the utilisation of idle or underemployed resources of all kinds. This sort of consideration affected the location of strategic industrial capacity in the United Kingdom in the 1930's. Apart from Northumberland and Durham, the areas of heavy unemployment on the coalfields were classified as relatively safe. The London region was considered to be exceptionally vulnerable and the Midlands 'unsafe'. The areas of economic distress thus combined what was considered to be a degree of safety with a pool of under-employed and often quite skilled labour and some pre-existing armament capacity. Thus small arms and explosives manufacture, and the aircraft industry, expanded production in these 'safe' regions, with Lancashire obtaining a good share. Concepts of what was a safe region were drastically altered by wartime experience, while acute shortages of labour soon became the dominant factor influencing location decisions during the war.[2]

The influence of such government-directed activity when war is imminent or actually in progress, however, spreads over into peacetime. While the output of munitions and weapons may be cut following the end of a war, the plants themselves may be taken over (often on very favourable terms) by private industry. In the United Kingdom, for example, 'the war left behind some 13 million square feet of munitions factory space which was suitable for taking over and adapting for the attraction of civilian industry to the Development Areas'.[3]

Further, the construction of war factories in a previously nonindustrialised area may well serve to create conditions conducive to the continuance of industrial activity in time of peace. For example, a previously unattractive labour situation may have been before building could begin. (We should note in passing that the prior permission of the local planning authority was also necessary before work could commence.) By the use of this method industrial development could be prevented at any point, while the application for a certificate enabled the Board of Trade to bring knowledge of the various locations available, and considered suitable, to the industrialist's attention.

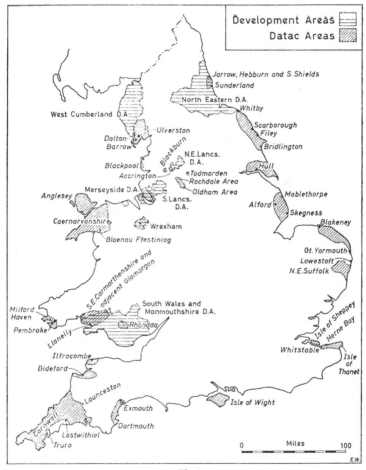

Fig 1
England and Wales. Development and DATAC Areas, 1959
(DATAC — Development Areas Treasury Advisory Committee)

Not all of these methods have been acted upon vigorously. Development of the services mentioned in paragraph 3 above has lagged, especially perhaps in the improvement of roads, and little fundamental research seems to have been carried out. In the long term, the most important method of locational control proved to be the IDC.

The Distribution of Industry Act defined the Development Areas—broadly the Special Areas of the 1930's with considerably enlarged boundaries, which contained, in 1939, some 6,500,000 people. Additions to these areas were made subsequently: Wrexham and the Wigan–St Helen's area in 1946, Merseyside in 1949 and north-east Lancashire in 1953, while the Scottish Development Area came to include part of the Highlands. (Fig. 1 shows these Development Areas in England and Wales.) The aim was to use the methods described above to influence industrialists in their choice of location, and thus to achieve an influx of a wider range of industrial employment into the Development Areas. The main burden of applying this policy was laid upon the Board of Trade, which was to work with Local Planning Authorities (the councils of Counties and County Boroughs). 'The Board of Trade is responsible for location in the wider sense, while Local Planning Authorities are responsible for siting in the strict sense, though no clear dividing line can be drawn between them.'[8]

The Board of Trade was given, through its control of the issue of IDCs, the task of persuading firms to set up, or expand their operations, in the Development Areas. At first an IDC was required for all industrial building exceeding 10,000 square feet in area, but this limit was soon lowered to 5,000 square feet.[9] The operation of official policy undoubtedly secured an influx of industry into the Development Areas beyond what would have taken place in its absence, although without examining each case individually it is not possible to ascertain exactly how much new capacity is directly the result of government activity. Table 8 (see p. 117) gives the results, in terms of employment, of industrial building schemes completed between 1945 and 1956 in Development Areas. In each case the population and the amount of government expenditure is also given. By 1958 the government was itself the landlord for between forty and fifty million square feet of factory space in Development Areas with over 1,000 tenants.[10]

At the same time the government's intention was to curb industrial expansion in Greater London and the Birmingham

TABLE 8

INDUSTRIAL BUILDING SCHEMES COMPLETED IN DEVELOPMENT AREAS, UK 1945 TO SEPTEMBER 1956

Development Area	Population 1954 (June)	Number of schemes	Additional employment provided Males	Females	Total	Expenditure by B.O.T. 1945–June 1957
	thousands					*£ million*
North-eastern	2,411	784	48,000	32,000	80,000	16·4
West Cumberland	158	68	4,000	2,000	6,000	1·8
South Wales and Mons.	1,741	553	40,000	25,000	65,000	21·1
Wrexham	89	31	400	100	500	0·8
South Lancs.	375	143	5,000	3,500	8,500	1·8
Merseyside	1,224	317	14,500	11,500	26,000	2·9
North-east Lancs.	180	64	3,000	2,000	5,000	1·6
Scottish D. Areas	2,642	830	42,000	26,500	68,500	24·8
Total	8,820	2,790	156,900	102,600	259,500	£71·2

Source: Board of Trade Journal, 2 August 1957

Based on IDCs, i.e. excludes buildings with under 5,000 sq. ft. of floor space. Employment estimates given by employers area. In practice this proved difficult, and, while the direction of industry to the Development Areas in the later 1940's had a good deal of success, the policy of preventing industrial expansion in the great conurbations of London and Birmingham proved economically less attractive in the 1950's. The Board of Trade was entrusted with the task of seeing that new industrial development was carried out 'consistently with the proper distribution of industry'. The critical questions are 'What *is* the proper distribution?' and 'By what criteria should it be measured?' The Board was also concerned to maintain a vigorous industrial economy in the country as a whole, for clearly regional prosperity depends in the final analysis on national prosperity. Changing economic conditions and the overriding claims of export industries served to emphasise the importance of the London and Birmigham areas in the national economy. These are the two most vigorous industrial regions in the country and they possess many attractions for a wide range of industry. They contain much of the country's potential in the new and growing industries, many of which produce important export items, and for some firms engaged in these industries expansion *in situ* is necessary. It is often difficult for them to move to other areas and the establishment of branch plants elsewhere is often a poor second best to expansion of the main works.

With growing competition in overseas markets in the 1950's, the varying costs of production in alternative locations needed more careful consideration. In the early post-war years conditions were uniquely favourable for the operation of Development Area policy. The post-war boom in demand and the continuous inflation enabled industrialists to pass on to the consumer whatever extra costs they incurred. The main objective was to get into production quickly to take advantage of the buoyant demand conditions, and here the inducements offered in the Development Areas, plus the availability of labour, often proved decisive. But from the early 1950's there was no longer a sellers' market for all types of goods. Purchasers were becoming more selective and more responsibe to changes in price, especially in overseas markets, where a revivified western Germany, among others, was competing ever more strongly. In such circumstances producers became more selective in their locational requirements and more applications were made for permission to expand in the official 'contraction' areas and fewer for the Development Areas. In the circumstances the Board of Trade had little option but to allow an increasing proportion of total industrial building to take place in the London and Birmingham regions.

Not all firms persuaded to move to the Development Areas were satisfied with the situation in which they found themselves, and some felt rather aggrieved that the less rigorous application of official policy subsequently allowed competing firms to slip into the areas of their own first choice (e.g. London or Birmingham) while they themselves had to face higher comparative costs. It was recognised that in steering industry to the Development Areas the Board of Trade was sometimes also steering it away from its most economic location. (This indeed is one reason why government assistance was made available.) Interim reports of studies by the National Institute of Economic and Social Research suggested that considerable increases in costs were sometimes incurred by firms which moved to Development Areas, and these had to be passed on to the consumer or absorbed.[11] Much of the new industrial capacity in Development Areas consists of branch plants of firms with their main centres of production elsewhere. According to Luttrell's early study of branch factories in the shoe manufacturing industry, initial extra costs could prove very high; the settling down period could be prolonged and management and supervisory difficulties raise costs substantially, while higher overheads could remain important for a long period.[12]

The case of a vehicle firm that was persuaded to set up a factory in the North-East Development Area, with the bait of ample labour and an available factory at low rent, is also interesting. First, the rent subsidy was not in perpetuity, and when the initial period was over the firm found its rent trebled to what was considered an 'economic' figure. This new financial burden was an addition to the comparative cost disadvantages that had arisen from certain difficulties inherent in the location. The main suppliers of materials were located in the Midlands and South, and the firm had to meet heavy delivery charges beyond those incurred by its competitors in those areas. The firm also felt remote from the centre of vehicle activity in the country and out of touch with current movements, exhibitions, conferences and so on. With these experiences behind it this firm would never have considered a location away from the Midlands or the south of England.[13] On the other hand, as a series of articles in the Board of Trade Journal suggest, many firms found their location requirement satisfactorily met in the Development Areas.[14] The obvious conclusion is that more needs to be known about the real locational requirements of individual industries so that the wrong type of industry is not persuaded to establish itself in a location that is for some reason receiving government assistance to attract industry.

The general picture of government activity and policy with regard to the location of industry in the recent past was complicated by the minor recession of 1958–9. This recession showed clearly that the pre-war depressed areas remained those where the effects of trade recession would be felt most strongly. The post-war increase of capacity in new industries in these Development Areas had certainly decreased the dependence of the Areas on a narrow range of industries, but not always by a substantial amount. The recession also brought into focus the fact that many other areas of the country possessed pockets of high unemployment. The general result was an apparently increased determination in government circles to use the 'stick and carrot' methods available to influence industrial location more rigorously. The IDC control was to be used more firmly, and financial assistance was, under the Distribution of Industry (Industrial Finance) Act of 1958, made more widely available. Projected industrial investment in many small places, called DATAC areas, from Cornwall to the Highlands and the islands of Scotland, could be assisted by the government (see Fig. 1).

The results of these powers were unspectacular and in 1960 new legislation (the Local Employment Act) replaced all previous enactments on employment policy. The new Act permitted the government to attract work to any locality where 'a high rate of unemployment exists or is imminent and likely to persist, whether seasonally or generally'.[15] By guiding industry to communities (called 'development districts') rather than to regions it was hoped to bring help directly to small areas in grave economic difficulties. Under the 1945 Act industrialists had often tended to select sites within the Development Areas at points where conditions were not at their most serious while the 'problem' districts had been largely avoided. Experience since 1960 has, however, confirmed early doubts on the validity of this new approach. The map of DATAC areas (Fig 1) shows many of the places that have appeared on government lists of Development Districts. Not all can realistically hope to attract viable manufacturing interests, while the geographical dispersal of effort that this policy entails means that limited resources can be too thinly spread to be really effective. Already, important modifications to the policy have been made in practice,[16] and it is unlikely that the Local Employment Act will pass through Parliament in its present form when it comes up for renewal in 1967. Be this as it may, whatever one may think of the nature, desirability and effectiveness of government activity in the sphere of industrial location, its significance in the United Kingdom is clear. The impact of such policies, however, is always more marked during times of rapid economic expansion than when the tempo of activity slackens.

Government influence on industrial location is also exercised in a factual way, in addition to the prohibitions and inducements that we have already discussed. The government has, of course, a direct control of the location of its own establishments (research stations and ordnance factories, for example) which can be located where it thinks fit. Social considerations (unemployment, for example) or strategic considerations may play an important part in the decision. Further, governments have control of nationalised industries in semi-socialist states such as our own. Here an attempt is sometimes made to remove the nationalised sector from the uncertainties of day to day politics by setting up independent boards to control them. The relations between these boards and the government are complex, but naturally the Minister to whom these boards are finally responsible must have a say in all important decisions, including those on location.

Certain other industries may also be subjected to stronger positive control of their affairs than is applied to industry in general, although they are not themselves nationalised. In the United Kingdom an important example is the iron and steel industry. Measures of public supervision of this industry date from the 1930's, through the British Iron and Steel Federation (a voluntary association of iron and steel makers) and the Import Duties Advisory Committee. At this time also the government intervened decisively, mainly on social grounds, in the location of a major new plant (Ebbw Vale). Since 1945, after several fluctuations, the public supervision of this industry, considered to be essential by all political parties, has come to rest with the Minister of Power. He works largely through the Iron and Steel Board, which in turn has a duty to 'promote the efficient, economic and adequate supply under competitive conditions of iron and steel products'. Its chief powers with regard to location are the power to veto any major development scheme proposed by the industry, and to recommend the Minister to undertake any necessary development project which the industry itself is unwilling to carry out. These powers naturally give it a strong control over the

location of projected new capacity. In fact, however, the location
of this industry, with its manifold ramifications and effects on
other industries, is considered to be so important that major
decisions are often taken by the Cabinet itself. A recent example
is the Cabinet decision to split a steel strip mill development project into two portions. The company concerned wished to locate
the entire project in south Wales, but after protracted debate the
new capacity was split between south Wales and Scotland, the
Scottish participation being again based mainly on social grounds.

Other UK industries have also been the subject of special government interest and activity, with important locational implications.
Thus, the geographical pattern of motor vehicle manufacture in
1965 differs significantly from that of 1960. A large new centre of
vehicle manufacture has appeared on Merseyside, and smaller
centres in central Scotland and south Wales. These new locations
owe their origin solely to government intervention in the investment and location decisions of vehicle manufacturers.[17] In a
different field, a very large direct loan from the government has
supported the building of a big new pulp and paper mill at Fort
William in Scotland; while the 'new look' of the UK cotton
industry derives directly from the Cotton Industry Act of 1959,
which financed a controlled contraction of this long-ailing industry, and provided grants for the re-equipping of mills remaining in the business.

In this chapter we have considered briefly the large problem of
governmental influence on the location of industry, and have
given sufficient instances to show that even outside the Communist countries (where not merely the location but also the ownership and management of industry are wholly vested in the
government) governments take a large and increasing share in
deciding the location of industry. Motives, aims, powers and
methods in exercising governmental control vary from one country
to another, but it is safe to say that in no country now are industrialists completely independent of political decisions in making their own decisions about location.[18]

[1] S. E. Harris, *The Economics of New England*, 1952, ch. 20

[2] See W. Hornby, *Factories and Plant* (*History of the Second World War*),
1958

[3] Dame Alix Meynell, 'Location of Industry', *Public Administration*, Spring
1959

[4] *Economic Geography*, January 1953

[5] B. Martin, 'Conservative Labour Patterns in Japan', *Current History*, August 1959, p. 89

[6] Report of the Royal Commission on the Geographical Distribution of the Industrial Population, *CMD 6153*, 1940

[7] White Paper on Employment Policy, *CMD 6527*, 1944

[8] Town and Country Planning 1943–51, *CMD 8204*, p. 86

[9] In 1965 the limit was reduced to 1,000 square feet.

[10] Dame Alix Meynell, op. cit.

[11] D. C. Hague and P. K. Newman, *Costs in Alternative Locations: the Clothing Industry*, 1952; W. F. Luttrell, *The Cost of Industrial Movement*, 1952

[12] Op. cit.

[13] See letter 'Too Big for Their Bounds' in the *Economist*, 10 December 1955

[14] See *Board of Trade Journal*, 14 August 1959, et seq.

[15] *Local Employment Act*, 1960

[16] For e.g. practically the whole of Durham county is now covered by Development Districts. This procedure has had the effect of restoring a 'regional' approach to matters of location in areas of economic difficulty, and permits the new enthusiasm for encouraging maximum development at well selected 'growth points' to be more effectively indulged

[17] See R. C. Estall, 'New Locations in Vehicle Manufacture', *Town and Country Planning*, March 1964

[18] For a discussion of the situation in the USA see R. C. Estall, 'Planning for Industry in the Distressed Areas of the USA', *Journal of the Town Planning Institute*, November 1964

7

OTHER INFLUENCES ON INDUSTRIAL LOCATION

The earlier chapters have discussed those forces that are of major importance in relation to the broader aspects of the location decision, that is, to the choice of region in which to establish a plant. This is especially significant in a large country; but within a satisfactory region the industrialist will normally wish to find a satisfactory community and a satisfactory site. This postulates the existence of two levels in the location decision—the broader regional level and the narrower local level—and for many industries the choice will indeed be made in the two relevant stages. But the line of division between these two levels of decision is not always clearly defined. For some producers stringent local requirements, especially perhaps with regard to the site, could even affect the decision as to area or region. Local features are therefore of considerable importance, and will be treated under the separate headings of 'sites and services', 'promotional activities of local bodies', 'local taxation' and 'water supply'. Another influence yet to be mentioned is that of climate, which is also discussed in the present chapter.

Sites and services

Actual *site* requirements of certain manufacturing enterprises are often quite exacting, and the lack of the necessary qualities of site can sometimes cause an otherwise very promising general location to be ruled out. Many industrial processes require a large area of level land for single storey lay-out. It may be necessary, further, for the site to be alongside a water artery or railway, which may restrict the number of possible sites in any given locality. Road requirements are even more important to many modern industries, but their absence is generally more easily remedied. A firm may also want ample space for later expansion, thus making its land requirements more difficult to satisfy. Some industrial buildings, with their equipment, impose heavy loads upon their foundations and so the local geology may limit the choice of sites. Yet others require enormous quantities of water and their thirst can be satisfied only by a location near a large river or lake or the sea. The choice of site is further complicated if the process gives rise to a liquid or solid waste or greatly heats its cooling water before discharge, to the detriment of other interests in the vicinity. Among the highly important industries affected in their site requirements by such considerations are modern integrated iron and steel works, oil refineries, heavy chemical works, automobile and aircraft assembly plants.

The availability of suitable sites may be further restricted by local planning authority activity. In the United Kingdom all forms of industrial development require the permission of the local planning authority, as well as the IDC from the Board of Trade that was discussed in Chapter 6. A refusal by the planning authority of permission to develop a given site may cause the firm concerned to seek a location elsewhere. There have been important cases of this type in the United Kingdom in recent years. For some kinds of manufacturing activity, too, the type of development around a prospective site may be important. Thus the manufacture of high-quality drugs, such as penicillin, must be carried on under aseptic conditions which demand clean air, and surrounding development needs to be considered from the point of view of air pollution. No modern food or drugs firm would be content with a site in the vicinity of a cement works, for example.

For many industries the price of the land, or conditions of rental, must also be considered, although for the large organisation these costs are normally small in relation to total costs and are therefore almost negligible as a locating influence. Within an industrial centre, however, the price of land may well influence the precise distribution of industries of various types. These few points serve to illustrate the importance of the availability of suitable sites in an area considered generally favourable from other points of view.

The availability of suitable *buildings* may also be relevant. This was particularly significant in the earlier post-war years, when a producers' market stimulated many industries to immediate expansion. The stumbling block often lay in the lack of premises, and the building industry itself was in many countries fully occupied with other urgent work. Building materials and labour were also in short supply in some instances. The existence of even approximately suitable premises was therefore a strong attraction and, as we have seen, certain areas possessed wartime factories no longer required for defence work. Although the location might be one where production costs were greater than elsewhere (at least initially), the incentive of immediate production caused these war factories to become highly desirable property in many localities. In the circumstances higher costs could be readily passed on in higher prices. Garwood's analysis of post-war migration to Utah and Colorado showed, for example, that the two largest firms in the study located in Colorado because former government installations were made available to them.[1] Similar experiences are recorded in *Why Industry Moves South*.[2] In the United Kingdom many Royal Ordnance Factories became the nuclei of Trading Estates.

The availability of *services* is also a considerable factor in the actual siting decision. A prospective manufacturer will be encouraged by the suitable provision of such things as electric power and water supplies, adequate refuse disposal facilities, efficient fire and police services, good highway maintenance, and satisfactory transport services. If the locality has deficiencies in such services, the willingness and ability to remedy them quickly will be of importance. In a choice between suitable locations, which is not uncommon, superior community facilities for education, recreation and so on will make one area more attractive. This may be particularly important when a branch plant is being established at a distance from the parent plant and it is necessary to attract key workers to the new location.

Among other features that affect the attraction of a given locality is the *size of the community*. Some firms prefer a smaller community, where they are able to dominate the local employment structure. They claim that thereby they gain in the general attitude to employment, while the employees (and indeed the whole community) have a stake in the success of the business. On the other hand many firms prefer a large community, where a variety of general services is available, where component parts and productive services can be obtained from specialist firms and where labour supply is, as we have seen, more flexible.

Local attitudes to a prospective new industry can also influence the final choice of location. Manufacturers are understandably anxious to avoid a location where the community's attitude is unfriendly or hostile. A co-operative attitude by local leaders adds to any other attractions a location may possess.

Promotional activities of local bodies

Efforts by local bodies to attract new industries may take one of two broad forms. First, some form of financial help may be promised. Such financial inducements, themselves take various forms, for example outright money gifts, the offering of sites rent free or at artificially low rents, or local tax exemption. The attitude of industrialists to such inducements varies. Some accept money donations 'as an expression of community feeling'.[3] Others fear that acceptance carries a risk that a body making a substantial financial contribution might want to interfere with management.[4] The possibility of local tax exemption for a period of years, however, or of obtaining a site at a purely nominal rent must surely be a temptation to entrepreneurs, especially perhaps those with small businesses. In certain industries in the United States acceptance of financial inducements in various forms from local bodies appears to be the rule rather than the exception. Examples are the shoe industry and the garment industry.[5]

Secondly, in order to promote increased industrial activity local bodies often provide information about their areas. The information gathered usually results from programmes of research into the advantages offered to industry by the locality. The availability of such information saves industrialists from expending time and money on their own private research into a prospective location. The results of the research are used to advertise the advantages of the location, either for a wide range of industry or for a particular type of enterprise. It may be safe to assume that really large firms are in the main unaffected by such advertisement, and prefer to assess the prospects of alternative locations themselves. Smaller firms may, however, be strongly influenced and be led to enquire more closely into the possibilities of a site in the area in question. Without doubt the availability of published and unpublished material relative to the resources and economic condition of a locality can be of great value to industry. Organisations known to be gathering, arranging and interpreting such data are often approached by manufacturers for advice and assistance in location problems.

Promotional activities of this kind are in the hands of official, semi-official or private bodies, whose areas of promotional activity range from regional to local. In the United Kingdom such bodies as the Scottish Council (Development and Industry) and the Lancashire and Merseyside Industrial Development Association have been providing useful studies of, and information on, their regions for some years. Recently the promotional activities of the Northern Ireland Development Council have impinged on the consciousness of every serious newspaper reader as the Council has sought to present the advantages of Northern Ireland to prospective industrialists. Countries currently undergoing the process of industrialisation of their economies undertake promotional activities on a national level, sponsored by the government or by private organisations. Thus banking interests in Australia provide industrial surveys and reports on possible locations to prospective enterprises, and produce handbooks discussing market potential, the provision of basic services and resources, labour issues, taxation and so on.[6] In the United States almost every region possesses promotional organisations which co-operate with, and co-ordinate the activities of, state associations of manufacturers, development commissions, local chambers of commerce and other associations. As suggested above, the most valuable work done by such bodies is in the provision of information.

'A growing number of manufacturers are basing location decisions on careful investigation of more and more factors which have a bearing on the decision. They are searching for increased amounts of local economic data and are evaluating community attitudes towards industry more carefully. Several development corporations, as well as other industrial development groups, are compiling and presenting the types of local information manufacturers want. . . . The existence of a local development corporation is evidence of a receptive attitude towards manufacturers and willingness to help them.'[7]

Local taxation

Tax variations within national or regional boundaries may also affect location decisions. Tax concessions may be deliberately used by local authorities to attract industry, and this device has been popular in the southern states of the USA. Significant tax variations are often found in federal states, as was seen in Chapter 6. The Federal Government itself is normally concerned to maintain even taxation over the whole country—except where 'zone allowances' are used, as in Australia, to encourage development in remoter parts. But state governments have their own tax structures and, within the state, local areas again apply local taxes or rates. In the United States, industry is taxed not only at the federal but also at state and local levels. In the incidence of taxation on industry and industrialists there are therefore substantial geographical variations, with consequent effects on location decisions. Massachusetts has already been quoted as an example of an area adversely affected by a high tax reputation. (See Chapter 6.)

Local governments, as distinct from national, therefore face a dilemma. Numerous and efficient services must be provided if industry is to be attracted at all, but a high level of taxes to pay for these services is apt to deter industrialists. We should, however, keep this matter in perspective. 'Do state and local taxes play a *dominant* role in the location decisions of most important business firms? Our conclusion is they do not. . . . Does this mean that taxes play no role in location? No, for sometimes taxation may be that marginal element which tips the scale in favour of a certain location.'[8]

Water supply

The fact that this material requirement of industry is being treated so late has no significance—unless it be to emphasise its importance. Water is an essential requirement of all industrial plant and a vital raw material in many, being used variously in processing, in steam raising and in cooling. The industrial use of water has grown very rapidly in this century, and several United Nations publications have suggested that the use of water *per capita* outside of agriculture could be a good index of standards of living. Be this as it may, the increasing thirst of modern industry makes the satisfaction of water requirements a serious matter in location decisions. In the United States it has been estimated[9] that an average of 40 thousand million gallons of water were used per day in 1900, but by 1960 the amount had risen to about 320 thousand million, an eightfold increase in sixty years. Estimates for 1980 assess total daily consumption at about 500 thousand million gallons. Of these totals, industry and steam-generated electricity stations consumed some 37 per cent in 1900, and 50 per cent in 1960. They could increase their share of the total to some 60 per cent or more by 1980. Throughout this section 'industrial use' of water will be taken as including water used in steam-generated electricity stations, except where otherwise stated. Water used in hydro-electric power generation, however, is excluded from

E

water-use statistics, since these stations do not use water in the same sense as industry and steam stations.

There are several variables to be considered in assessing the importance of water in location decisions. The first variables are in supply, that is in the quantity and quality of available resources. Obviously the quantity of water available varies from area to area and seasonally within a given area. The number of possible locations for industrial enterprise in a given region may be severely restricted by overall or seasonal water shortage. This is especially true for those industries with large water requirements, and such industries are often the fundamental ones in an industrial economy. The supply of water also varies in its sources, which may be either surface or underground. Surface water is generally inferior, containing dissolved oxygen, organic matter and other impurities. Underground water is thus preferred for some uses, despite possibly higher fixed and operating costs incurred in exploiting it. But surface water is more widely obtainable in the quantities required and thus most industrial demands (e.g. c. 75 per cent in the United States) are met from surface sources.

This consideration of ground and surface supplies is associated with another variable in water supply, which is that the quality of water (surface or underground) varies from area to area. The importance of this will be emphasised below. At the moment we may note that poor quality water can be upgraded by various treatments. This might be an unwarranted addition to total development and operating costs that could be avoided in a different location. Often, however, minor deficiencies or undesirable properties can be countered by simple and inexpensive treatment. It is true that even good water may be spoilt locally by waste disposal, which charges the water with organisms and other impurities expensive to remove. Industries requiring pure water will therefore examine the methods of liquid effluent disposal in the vicinity of a prospective location.

The second group of variables is in demand, and again concerns variations in the quantity and the quality of water requirements. Clearly there are enormous variations between industries in the quantity needed. For example, the 769 establishments engaged in primary metal manufacture in the United States in 1959 took 30 per cent of the total water intake by industry (excluding electricity generation) in the country.[10] On the other hand, textile mills, for which water is also a very important material, used just over 1 per cent of the national total in 511 establishments. Such statistics do not necessarily reflect efficient use of the water. Users in the main industrial areas of the United States, where water is normally abundant and cheap, have little incentive to incur extra expense in using it efficiently. Most large users, however, do circulate much of their water, using it several times and thus decreasing their total intake requirements. In fact the total water required by industry in the United States would be almost doubled if no water was re-circulated.

Only a small fraction of all water used is actually consumed, i.e. incorporated into the product or lost to evaporation or in other ways. Much of the vast quantity used for cooling, steam raising, washing and so on can be used again and again, thus reducing the 'make-up' requirements. This is especially important for cooling water, which is the largest single use to which water is put by industry, taking about one-half of total industrial water used in the United States, and, to select another example in very different circumstances, about 43 per cent in Norway.[11] Where supplies are really abundant, cooling water may be used only once, and the firm saves the cost of land, buildings, equipment and staff which would be required for cooling installations. In many cases, however, water is not in such lavish supply, and various devices are used to cool the water and reduce evaporation and other losses. Cooling towers can save over 90 per cent of the water and thus reduce considerably the total quantities withdrawn from the source.

Water requirements for other uses in industry are generally relatively small. Modern steam-raising equipment uses water most efficiently, condensing the steam and re-using, and often requires only about 2 per cent of make-up water.[12] Processing requirements vary greatly. Cooking, dyeing or rinsing, for example, may need considerable quantities; while much 'process water' may be needed for washing product or material or for technical purposes. Some industries incorporate water into the product, as, for example, beverages and many food and chemical products. There are many other demands for water in industrial establishments, for sanitary purposes, air-conditioning and humidifying and so on; but such miscellaneous requirements form in aggregate a small proportion of the total.

Table 9 shows the water intake for selected manufacturing industries in the United States in 1959. The figures are not intended to be typical of the industry groups to which the selected industries belong, but are given as a cross-section of industry types, with variations in quantities taken or proportions treated or used in various ways. By far the largest consumer class is that of the 'blast furnaces and steel mills', but other very large water users include petroleum refining and paper mills, while in average quantity per establishment primary aluminium manufacture has the largest intake. Of these prolific water users, the blast furnaces and steel mills and petroleum refineries require truly vast quantities for cooling purposes, whereas in paper mills the greatest demand is for process water and in primary aluminium plant almost four-fifths of the total intake is for steam electricity generation. The satisfaction of the thirst of these industries is not always easy, and water supply can become an important locational consideration, certainly affecting the actual choice of district and site within a region that is otherwise generally satisfactory. Satisfaction may be yet more difficult where water *quality* is also of great importance, as it is in paper manufacture.

Variations in quantity demanded can be impressively stated as water requirements per unit of product, and a few examples may be of interest. In the United States, steel typically requires about 65,000 gallons per ton produced, paper made from wood some 38,000 gallons and rayon fibre about 220,000 gallons, while thermal electricity production consumes some 8,000 gallons per kilowatt-hour.[13] For smaller-scale industries we may take examples from Belgium,[14] where about 3,300 gallons of water are required on average per ton of raw fruit canned and some 5 to 20 gallons of water per gallon of beer or lemonade produced.

Variations in quality of the water required are also considerable. Water varies considerably in smell and taste, in turbidity (suspended matter), in corrosive and scale-forming qualities, in temperature, conductability, clogging power and in other ways. These variations, singly or in combination, may be important to the industrial user. Fortunately the very large quantities required for cooling purposes need not be of high grade. The main requirement is that its temperature be low. A certain amount of prior treatment, however, especially of surface water, may be required to remove undesirable impurities or corrosive properties; but Table 9 confirms that where a large proportion of total water intake is used for cooling purposes, as in iron and steel manufacture and petroleum refining, the proportion treated prior to use is small.

By contrast water for steam raising in modern high-pressure boilers needs to be quite pure. Suspended solids must be removed and scale-forming and corrosive properties reduced since incrustation and corrosion proceed faster in modern boilers than in the

TABLE 9

WATER USE IN SELECTED INDUSTRIES, USA 1955

	Total intake (billion gallons*)	Per cent treated prior to use	Type of use, per cent				Per cent treated prior to discharge	Number of establishments
			Process	Cooling and condensing	Steam electricity generation	Boiler and misc.		
All manufacturing	12,175	16	26	46	21	8	20	7,720
Blast furnaces and steel mills	2,994	12	26	45	24	5	16	213
Petroleum refining	1,311	11	6	84	3	6	55	215
Paper mills	1,089	44	64	6	26	5	21	211
Primary aluminium	177	6	4	6	79	9	9	16
Sawmills and planing mills	120	4	20	7	60	14	26	86
Motor vehicles and parts	125	12	26	20	1	54	13	260
Meat packing plants	76	16	45	36	1	18	16	162
Finishing textiles (cotton)	51	63	76	2	14	8	20	54
Canned food specialities	15	53	60	27	—	13	15	33
Leather tanning and finishing	12	10	83	8	—	8	18	60
Photographic equipment	11	64	64	27	—	9	60	13

Source: US Census of Manufactures 1958 Vol. 1. Data for establishments with intake of 20 million gallons or more

* In the USA one billion equals a thousand million

robust, but inefficient, nineteenth-century boilers that operated at pressures below 100 lb per square inch. Further, the expense of modern boiler plant means that it must be kept continuously at work. Boilers cannot frequently be permitted to go out and cool for scaling and cleaning, which was the practice with low-pressure equipment. Thus the tolerance for hardness (which affects scale deposition) varies from 75 parts per million for boilers working at pressures below 150 lb per square inch, to 8 parts per million where operating pressures are over 250 lb.[15] The quality of the water for steam-raising is therefore very important. Natural water supply is not always pure enough and the necessary treatments add to operating expenses.

The quality requirement for process water will vary according to the actual use. Water used for washing the product in steel works, for example, need not be very pure. Conversely, where the water actually enters an edible product the highest standards must apply, as in food and drink manufacture and the production of drugs. Here turbidity, colour, smell, taste and mineral content are all of vital importance. In the manufacture of beverages local waters can become relatively well known (or advertised) because of some real or supposed excellence of quality. Most beer drinkers in the United Kingdom know of the Burton brew, and in the United States 'Rocky Mountain Waters' are well advertised for their brewing qualities. In historic times the waters of the Thames were considered of high quality—so desirable in fact that Thames water was taken in barrels to Lisbon for brewing! It seems incredible when we look at London's sewer today.

High standards of purity may also be required where the process water does not enter the product in the same way. The manufacture of photographic equipment, for example, demands water of high quality, as do paper manufacture and many textile processes. Table 9 shows that the photographic equipment, paper mill and textile-finishing industries treat a very large proportion of their total intake prior to use, and this may be taken as a rough guide to the need for high quality water.

Although there is a dearth of useful statistical material, we must comment briefly on the costs of water supply. In general, as we have stated, water is regarded as a cheap commodity. And, indeed, it has to be, given its use in such vast quantities. The actual costs incurred will vary widely according to location and site, reflecting, for example, the presence or absence of a local source, the need for purification and re-cycling, the costs of pumping and storing and the necessity of treating waste effluents. Generally, however, water costs form a low proportion of total costs in industry as a whole. But this is primarily because industry has in fact usually located where water is cheap. No firm could lightly undertake operations in an area where water supply was difficult and abnormally costly.

As between industries, however, the proportion of water costs to total costs will naturally vary according to particular requirements and conditions of supply.

'A cost for water that is permissible in one industry may be far in excess of what another industry can afford. A plant such as a petroleum refinery or a steel mill, using large quantities of water per unit of production, must have a low-cost water supply. Industries using only small quantities of water per unit of high-priced product, on the other hand, can stand relatively high-cost water for selective uses. . . .'[16]

The latter types of industry therefore have more freedom in their choice of location.

In concluding this section we may indicate some wider issues. Individual industries may, as we have seen, be restricted in their choice of location by their needs for water. But many industries tend to gather together in large concentrations where they hope to reap advantages of the type discussed in Chapter 5. Such large industrial concentrations lead to heavy demand for water not only for the industries, but also for the associated concentration of people and services. The supply of these industrial, domestic and municipal needs may raise serious problems and create one of the dis-economies of concentration to which we have referred. Deficiencies in water supply, set against increasing requirements and the inconvenience and expense of carrying water over long distances by pipeline, may well eventually put an upward limit on the size of certain great conurbations. On a rather smaller scale the problem has already become acute in the Witwatersrand conurbation. Here, water supplies were one of the original attractions for industry, but the combined needs of mines, industries and domestic consumers have outgrown the supply. Despite measures taken in the late 1950's to double water storage capacity, the Natural Resources Development Council recommended that no large industrial users of water should be permitted to locate themselves in the Vaal River Basin, unless there are compelling 'geographical reasons'.[17]

An associated problem is the disposal of liquid waste, serious wherever there are large users of water, but doubly so in large urban-industrial concentrations. Table 9 shows that only some 20 per cent of all water discharged by industrial users in the United States in 1959 was given prior treatment. Not all industrial waste is noxious, but that which is affects other interests, especially downstream of the discharge. The discharge of large quantities of cooling water at high temperatures raises the temperature of water in a river and affects many other users. Thus waste-disposal practices of upstream users can have an effect on the location decision of a firm, for it might be involved in unnecessary fixed and operating expenditure for water treatment prior to use. One obstacle to the improving of this situation is that firms are reluctant to spend money on waste treatment plant that primarily benefits downstream users. The disposal of liquid effluent can become a very serious and expensive matter. A food products factory locating itself in the Wigan area in the United Kingdom had assured itself first that Wigan could supply it with the $4\frac{1}{4}$ million gallons of water per day that it would eventually need. The extension to the existing water-supply facilities that were required cost Wigan about £400,000. But the vegetable effluent from this plant will eventually reach some three million gallons per day, and in extending their sewage works Wigan spent half as much again as it had spent on the water-supply project.[18]

The need for water, then, can be a very important consideration in the location of industry. The 'pull' of water supply is naturally greater in regions where water is not abundant. The major industrial concentrations of our time are to be found, however, mainly in temperate latitudes where cyclonic or orographic influences on precipitation are strong. Water supply was thus never an acute problem. As industrial activity grows in other areas of the world, however, in Australia or Monsoon Asia for example, or in the drier regions of countries already well advanced along the industrial road, water may play a greater part in the location decision. The President's Materials Policy Commission in the United States concluded: 'By 1975, access to good water may become the most important factor in deciding where to locate industries.'[19] This could be an over-statement of enthusiastic water engineers, but it may well contain more than a grain of truth.

Climate and location

We now turn to another influence of the physical environment. The importance of climate, directly, to the agricultural and tourist industries is evident, and climate (especially relative extremes of cold and heat and shortage of water) has an obvious effect on the mineral extraction industry, as for example at Knob Lake or Kalgoorlie. Its role in the location of manufacturing activity may not be so obvious, however, and some treatment of the matter is desirable here.

Extreme conditions would in general prohibit most forms of economic activity, including manufacturing. But in this context we are not normally concerned with extreme conditions. Just because of that, the part played by climate is difficult to measure. Some of the well-worn correlations, e.g. that the climate of Lancashire played the fundamental part in the location there of the cotton industry, have to be dismissed for the over-simplifications that they are. Nevertheless, to a certain extent climate will be reflected in costs and in a variety of intangible and immeasurable ways. Some geographers have considered that climate plays an important part in the development of nations, affecting as it does the energy of, and the stimulus given to, man in his various environments. There may be some truth in this contention, but within the range of choice open to most manufacturers, climate probably plays a relatively small role. It is, however, possible to indicate various ways in which climate may have some effect on industrial activity and location:

1. In some types of industry the location decision can be quite rigorously affected by climatic considerations. This is obviously true of some processes using the produce of agriculture directly. Since climate affects the type and productivity of agriculture it will naturally affect the location of, for instance, industries engaged in preserving or canning fresh foods. The distribution of the aircraft industry in the USA also reflects climatic conditions. The manufacture of aircraft engines and propellors is heavily concentrated in the north-east. Airframe production and final assembly, however, are mainly located in the south-west, where the mild climate permits much work to be carried on out of doors, allows all-year flying and enables parts and equipment to be stored safely and cheaply in the open. Further, the mild winters reduce heating needs—very important where the workshops cover millions of square feet of floor space.[20]

2. Regions with periods of intense heat normally experience a fall in productivity during the hot spells. This can either be accepted, and output lost, or be combated by the installation of air-conditioning equipment, with extra costs for the installation

and operation of the equipment. In cold regions extra costs are incurred for heating apparatus and its operation, while outside work can be completely stopped by excessive cold. Thus work on shipbuilding is interrupted in north-east USA during very cold spells in winter. Conversely, shipbuilding can be affected temporarily in the same centres in summer by periods of great heat, which makes work on the metal ships unbearable. In this context we may note that the north-western states of USA are more suited climatically for such outdoor operations, and shipbuilding is rarely interrupted by either summer heat or winter cold. We are not surprised, therefore, to see a relative increase of shipbuilding in the north-west over the past two decades.

Even in a temperate zone such as ours, climate can influence manufacturing activity sporadically. Hot spells can cause a suspension of work in certain food-processing plants, as when in chocolate-product factories the chocolate will not set. This sort of climatic influence in our country, however, plays little serious part in location decisions. In general an equable climate is most favourable to industrial activity, since operations can be carried on continuously throughout the year, thus permitting, among other things, the spreading of fixed (overhead) costs over a greater number of units of output.

3. Excessive heat can damage the permanent way on railways, and can also increase the time, and thus the costs, of road journeys. At the other end of the scale, ice and snow can interrupt normal traffic flow by water, land and air and slow up manufacturing output. The winter of 1946–7 in the United Kingdom was of such severity as to cause serious interference with industrial activity—largely because the movement of coal by rail was interrupted. This experience was abnormal in this country, but where such conditions are normal the costs to the local community of maintaining and operating large snow-removal and de-icing equipment can also affect the costs of individual firms.

4. A further aspect is that areas highly favoured climatically are attractive to people. As their population grows such areas become progressively attractive to industry. A recent American newspaper report illustrates how the necessary labour can often be readily attracted to a climatically favoured area. Precisely similar jobs were advertised in the same firm with works in the north-east and in Florida. While the firm had numerous inquiries about the Florida post, only a few routine inquiries were received about the other. On a larger scale the attractiveness of the climate

goes far to explain the spectacular growth of population and of manufacturing industry in southern California.

5. Climate is also reflected in the habits and requirements of consumers, and thus affects the prospects for consumer goods industries of various types. There will obviously be a relatively small market in Florida for home-heating appliances, while the market for prefabricated swimming-pools in Nova Scotia will also be relatively restricted.

6. Climate may also affect the industrial process itself. Where natural conditions are not as good as would ideally be required the requisite conditions can often be provided artificially—at a certain additional cost, which may or may not be important. Thus artificial humidifiers are used, especially for fine textile work, where the air is normally or periodically too dry. An interesting case of a climatic advantage in processing gained entirely unexpectedly was found by Garwood in his study of industrial migration to Utah and Colorado:[21] a producer of aluminium pistons who migrated to Utah for entirely different reasons found that the low humidity was a helpful factor in avoiding gas pockets in the product, a feature that causes a high percentage of rejections in the Great Lakes area.

The comments on climate in Garwood's article are interesting. About a quarter of the firms studied stated that climate was the main reason for their location in Utah or Colorado, not because of its contribution to production but because the owners and operators wished to live there. Naturally the industries concerned were those in which no factor of production had an overwhelming pull. The labour requirements were relatively small (average twelve workers), and clothing, mattress manufacture, stationery and furniture were among the chief industries represented. Even so, these producers probably have had to accept higher costs, smaller markets and poorer prospects than they might have had in other locations. 'Personal' considerations (including climate) are also recorded as playing a very important part in the attraction of new manufacturing enterprise to Arizona in recent years. But it would appear, again, that most of the establishments whose location can be ascribed predominantly to such non-economic factors are of small size. The major industries in this still quite minor industrial state were located there for very different reasons.[22] Personal considerations, unsupported by economic advantages of any kind, can hardly weigh heavily where a major industry is concerned, or where the entrepreneur has as a main aim the maximisation of profit margins. The charm of a pleasant climate, that is to say, may be important where no essential requirement, or group of requirements, pulls the industry strongly to a certain type of location. In most cases, however, it will be a marginal consideration that may tip the balance between two or more locations equally attractive from the point of view of production costs.

[1] *Economic Geography*, January 1953

[2] McLaughlin and Robock, op. cit.

[3] Garwood, op. cit.

[4] *Why Industry Moves South*, op. cit., p. 112

[5] Ibid.

[6] For example, *The Establishment of Industry in Australia*, published by the Australian and New Zealand Bank Ltd., 1958

[7] Federal Reserve Bank of Boston, *Monthly Review*, January 1956

[8] National Planning Association, *The Economic State of New England*, 1954, p. 645. (Our italics)

[9] *U.S. Minerals Yearbook and Statistical Abstract of United States*, various years

[10] United States Department of Commerce, *Census of Manufactures*, 1958. Vol. I

[11] United Nations Department of Economic and Social Affairs, *Water for Industrial Use*, 1958

[12] Ibid.

[13] *U.S. Minerals Yearbook*, 1957, p. 1277

[14] Calculated from United Nations, *Water for Industrial Use*, 1959, op. cit., table 4

[15] Ibid., table 7

[16] Ibid., p. 11

[17] M. M. Cole, 'The Witwatersrand Conurbation. A Watershed Mining and Industrial Region', *Transaction of the Institute of British Geographers*, 1957

[18] A note on 'Effluent Disposal and Industrial Geography', by J. R. Gibson, appears in *Geography*, 1958

[19] The President's Materials Policy Commission, *Resources for Freedom*, 1952, vol. I, p. 50

[20] Alexandersson, op. cit., p. 58

[21] *Economic Geography*, 1953

[22] T. McKnight, 'Manufacturing in Arizona', *University of California Publications in Geography*, 1962. In fact, four large plants have played a key role in the growth of industrial employment and population (and, therefore, of the subsidiary and population-serving industries) in Arizona, and these four were located there for strategic reasons during World War II. In 1959 they still accounted for 27 per cent of all manufacturing employment in the state

8

SOME FINAL CONSIDERATIONS

We have now almost completed our broad survey of the physical, economic and social conditions that influence the patterns of industrial distributions. The treatment, while being far from exhaustive has, it is hoped, shown that, complex as the problem of location is, existing viable locations can normally be explained in terms of varying combinations of these major influences. We have not attempted to discriminate sharply between the historical problem of the location of existing enterprises and the present problem of locating new enterprises. Logically they are the same problem, but in practice there is a difference in that, thanks to the work of survey teams, national, regional and local, a considerable body of relevant information on prospective locations is nowadays available to industrialists planning new developments. We shall now give some attention to the discernible patterns of distribution in different industries.

Despite the complexity of individual location decisions, the wide regional variations in physical and economic conditions, and the existence of other pressures (especially of government activity) the typical patterns of location evolved in given industries often tend to be similar in different countries. This is broadly because certain economic and physical facts (and the physical facts here include not only features of the geographical environment but also the physical properties of the materials or the products, the physical nature of the processes and so on) often tend to be of overriding importance in the industry concerned. They tend therefore to give everywhere a general family resemblance in the patterns of distribution of any given industrial process.

Although the precise geographical pattern varies to an almost infinite degree from industry to industry, we may usefully distinguish three major types. First, there is the pattern provided by industries that are found in almost every sizeable urban centre. These are the 'ubiquitous' industries, distributed in much the same way as population itself. Secondly, and at the opposite end of the scale, there are industries in which a very large proportion of total capacity is limited to a few locations. These are the 'highly concentrated' industries. Between these there are processes in which some concentration is normal, but in which total capacity is more widely spread than in the highly concentrated group. These are the 'sporadic' industries. This threefold distinction is not hard and fast: some highly concentrated industries have their sporadic elements, for example, and some sporadic industries have their ubiquitous elements.

Examples of ubiquitous industries are not numerous and, with recent technical advances, especially in transport, they are tending to become fewer. Many service industries are, of course, ubiquitous, but we are not concerned with these in this book. A good example of a ubiquitous industry in manufacturing is baking, which occurs wherever there is a significant agglomeration of people. Another is the building industry. Alexandersson found that in 1950 only 10 per cent of all cities in USA had less than 4 per cent of their total employed population in the building industry.[1] Ice-cream manufacture, brewing and the manufacture of soft drinks may still be regarded as ubiquitous, though they are perhaps decreasingly so. Since the second world war they have shown a tendency towards production in larger, and consequently fewer, establishments. Nevertheless they remain widely dispersed because of the costs and difficulty of transporting the finished product.

High concentration is found in several important industries. Cotton textile manufacture, for example, is highly concentrated in Lancashire in the United Kingdom and, in the USA, in the southern Piedmont towns. In the United Kingdom, again, the manufacture of tin plate is highly concentrated in south Wales, jute manufacture in the Dundee area, pottery products in North Staffordshire. In the United States the fashion-clothing industry is heavily concentrated in New York City, the automobile industry in southern Michigan and adjacent portions of Ohio and Indiana, photographic equipment in New York State, and jewellery manufacture in Providence, Rhode Island. In all such industries, considerations of raw material supply, skilled labour requirements, the economies of agglomeration, of large-scale production, of market contacts and so forth have led almost inevitably to geographical patterns showing distinctive concentrations.

Between these two extremes, ubiquitous and highly concentrated, the patterns of distribution vary greatly from industry to industry, while the overlap into the concentrated and ubiquitous groups may also be considerable. Nevertheless, the sporadic pattern, though not always clear cut, is a common one. It is found, for example, in the furniture industry, in some metal-using industries—especially structural metal products and plumbing and heating equipment, in the manufacture of certain items of clothing such as shirts, in food canning and preserving, in wooden and cardboard box manufacture, and in the manufacture of light chemicals and certain rubber products.

Both the highly concentrated and the ubiquitous industries often possess sporadic elements, largely because of differences in the end product of different sections of the industry or differences in the market served. The fashion-clothing industry in the USA is certainly dominated by New York City and the Middle Atlantic States, but other branches of the clothing industry, men's clothing for example, are more widespread. Similarly, the automobile industry, though highly concentrated in southern Michigan and the adjacent areas of Indiana and Ohio, has a growing sporadic element in the final assembly stage of the finished vehicles. This dispersal is designed, among other things, to economise transfer costs by transporting the automobile in 'knocked-down' condition.

A good example of a ubiquitous industry with sporadic branches is the printing industry. The printing and publishing of books is chiefly a preserve of large metropolitan areas, which therefore possess a concentration of activity in this industry. But many small centres also print their own newspapers and provide printing facilities for other purposes, and the general pattern of distribution, therefore, is of an industry that is both sporadic and dispersed. Similarly, while the manufacture of bottled drinks is a widespread industry, it possesses its sporadic branches (e.g. whisky distilling) in which the product is of high value and can carry relatively high transfer costs.

Most modern industries, then, tend towards some degree of concentration in their distribution. The obvious reason is that, to a greater or lesser extent, they gain substantially from having a large, or very large, productive capacity in a given area. These gains may be obtained in various ways: by access to material or energy resources or to market, by the economies of agglomeration or industrial linkage, by the availability of labour skills and so forth—in fact by any of the means that have been discussed in the earlier chapters of this book. There is one further group of economies, however, of great importance in causing manufacturing industries to be, in varying degrees, concentrated geographically. These are the economies to be gained from large-scale production, and a separate treatment of this element is now desirable.

Scale of production

It is well known that by producing on a larger scale an entrepreneur may achieve many economies.[2] Maximum operating economies are obtained when the scale of production is large enough to permit every machine to be operated at its optimum output. This spreads the fixed overhead cost over the maximum units of product and so minimises the cost of each unit. Further savings are also made by buying and selling in very large quantities. Larger-scale operations may also make it possible to introduce better methods of production which could not be applied in a small establishment. The possibility of gaining substantial economies of these kinds is a strong incentive to the entrepreneur to adopt the largest practicable scale of operation. Clearly, the larger the prevalent size of plants in an industry the larger is the market that it can serve and the fewer the locations that are necessary.

Economies of large-scale production, however, may be readily obtainable in many industries in which the prevalent unit of production is small, for economies of scale in these industries can be more than offset by inconvenience and expense incurred in other ways. 'The [typical] unit of baking, of building, of ice manufacture is small not because economies of large-scale production do not exist, but because transport costs or transport difficulties prevent concentration of the industry into large units.'[3] In other words, where an industry serves a wide market with a product that is expensive or difficult to transport, or draws upon a widely available material, it may be desirable, or essential, to produce on a relatively small scale. No predictable pattern of location will follow inevitably from small size of plant. In the silk, textile and fashion-clothing industries, for example, production in small plants is normal because of rapid changes in style which put the very large plant, relying on economies from long runs of production of a single line, at a disadvantage. But these small plants gain substantially from geographical concentration. On the other hand there is a tendency for other industries in which the small plant dominates (as in baking, building and ice manufacture) to be geographically dispersed.

By contrast, when the production and marketing of a commodity can be most efficiently performed by an establishment of very large size, areal concentration of production often follows. The nature and size of the market is important here. A modern integrated iron and steel works, for example, probably achieves maximum economies of scale only when its output of rolled products falls between two and three million tons per annum. Not every location provides both a good assembly point for the raw materials and a ready market for such an output, and the industry therefore tends to be concentrated in relatively few locations. In the automobile industry large-scale operations bring substantial economies. In the United States many plants have an annual output of several hundred thousand cars. Such a scale of production needs a large market. Clearly there is a limit to the number of such plants required, and the main centres of the industry will tend to be located at a few favoured points.

Further examples of concentration are found in certain industries where economies of scale are considerable, but the total market is relatively small. In these industries most capacity will be concentrated in relatively few plants in relatively few locations. Ships, aircraft and locomotives are good examples of products of this kind. In some cases, again, the mechanisms of production are such that one large machine can satisfy the requirements of a very large community. A single match-making machine, for example, can cut match sticks sufficient to meet the needs of up to ten million people. One machine can blow bulbs for enough electric lamps to meet half the total demand in the United Kingdom, and so on. 'Even . . . if all the resources required for any kind of production were spread evenly throughout an area, we should not find all the kinds of production carried out in every part of the area; some of them would have to be localised simply because they can be carried out efficiently only on a large scale.'[4] Normally, of course, resources of all kinds are not evenly spread out and the centre of concentration will be at a point which has natural or acquired advantages of some kind to offer the industry.

In discussing this concept of scale and its significance in location patterns we have not in reality been introducing an entirely separate concept. It will be obvious that the prevalent size of plant itself is largely a function of the various forces that have been described earlier. The prevalent scale of production will have been influenced by such considerations as material supplies, access to and type of market, capital, management and labour considerations, historical influences, technological considerations and so on. We must here recall, however, that equally important economies in production can be achieved where a group of plants, separately controlled and not of the largest size, operate in juxtaposition, each being associated with the plants around it. Thus the geographical concentration of productive capacity in a given industry need not mean that output is mainly from large plants. It may mean a congregation of many small establishments which gain, as we have seen, from proximity to each other.

Location leaders

While we have seen that there are good reasons why a recognisable pattern of distribution should prevail in any given industry, we have as yet attempted no explanation of how the general pattern of distribution of all industry in a country might arise, i.e. how the pattern of distribution of the entire industrial population emerges and why it is as it is. There are in practice certain fundamental industries that are so important in their numbers of employees, or in the numbers and types of industries 'linked' with them, that they tend greatly to influence the main features of the distribution of industrial employment generally. Such major industries we may call the 'location leaders'. These are the industries on which a modern industrialised country's prosperity is usually based, and we may instance the iron and steel industry, heavy engineering, the heavy chemical industry, oil refining, aircraft manufacture and automobile production.

In such industries the question of location assumes added importance, for it is clearly not a matter of indifference where they are located. They normally involve extremely heavy capital investment and it would be unusual, to say the least, if a decision involving many millions of pounds were to be taken without a prolonged and serious assessment of the costs in alternative locations. The location decision is inevitably preceded by careful and detailed study of the influences we have discussed. In such industries, too, location is not always a 'once for all' business, as it is with many small enterprises. The search for and the assessment of a new location are conducted by men experienced in the requirements of their industry and with financial resources sufficient to command a series of detailed studies. It can be taken for granted, then, that industries of this kind are located where intensive investigation has indicated the maximum possible of locational advantage.

These are the type of industries that provide the framework for the general pattern of industrial distribution. They are large and important employers of labour, with all the associated advantages that this offers to other industries in their area; they provide a high proportion of earning (and therefore spending) capacity; they contribute significantly to the national total of value added by manufacturing industry; they are industries in which a considerable proportion of total new investment takes place. Table 10 gives some relevant statistics for five of these leading industries. In 1962 these provided over 13 per cent of total employment in manufacturing industry in the United States, about one-sixth of total earnings, one-fifth of total value added, and no less than a quarter of total investment in new plant and equipment.

Their leading role also arises naturally from the fact that they often provide the raw materials for, or use on an immense scale the products of, other industries and therefore powerfully attract them. It would be difficult to find an industrial process that did not use in some way the products of the iron and steel or chemical industries, while many firms exist partly or entirely to provide parts for use in the major assembly industry establishments. Such inter-industry relationships are admirably illustrated in 'input-output' tables for thirty-eight industry groups in UK.[5] The iron and steel (melting, rolling and casting) industry supplied 24 of the other 37 groups with products valued at £396 million. The chemicals group provided significant quantities of its products, valued at £119 million, to no fewer than 34 of them. On the other hand the motors and cycles group bought goods worth £207 million from 24 other groups. Not all the industries concerned would therefore necessarily be attracted to areas where iron and steel or chemicals are produced, or to the 'parent' assembly plant, but many are, and the influence of such location leaders on general distributions is profound. Further, the pattern set by the location leaders is often reinforced by the fact that many occupations and processes not essentially 'linked' with them are nevertheless attracted to the same locations by the concentration of industrial employment there and by the general economies of concentration that are available. They thus form the main nodes round which great industrial complexes have developed and they provide the underlying rationale of the geography of industrial activity.

TABLE 10

SIGNIFICANT STATISTICS FOR SOME LEADING INDUSTRIES, USA 1962

	Employment		Earnings		Value added by manufacture		New capital expenditure	
	thousands	*%*	*$ thousand million*	*%*	*$ thousand million*	*%*	*$ thousand million*	*%*
USA all manufacturing industry	16,766	100	94·3	100	179·3	100	10·4	100
Basic chemicals (organic and inorganic)	235	1·4	1·7	1·8	5·7	3·2	0·7	6·7
Petroleum refining	123	0·7	0·9	1·0	3·0	1·7	0·4	3·9
Blast furnaces and steel mills	502	3·0	3·6	3·8	6·6	3·7	0·7	6·7
Motor vehicles and equipment	667	4·0	4·7	5·0	11·6	6·5	0·5	4·8
Aircraft and parts	715	4·3	5·3	5·6	7·5	4·2	0·3	2·9
Total (5 industries)	2,242	13·4	16·2	17·2	34·4	19·2	2·6	25·0

Source: US Annual Survey of Manufactures, 1962
Percentage totals may be out because of rounding

It would be a mistake, however, to assume that the 'traditional' location leaders will everywhere provide a prime impetus to industrial development, and that the planned establishment of such enterprises will automatically trigger the processes of cumulative growth. These traditional leaders have flourished in their particular areas because of the suitability of those areas for their growth. In the attempt to stimulate industrial development in backward areas, however, they may well fail to secure a viable foothold in a reasonable period of time. A more fruitful impetus to rapid industrial growth in certain areas may be in supporting the integrated growth of a complex of linked or associated industries. Sophisticated input-output analysis of established complexes in advanced industrial areas has identified combinations of closely associated industries. Such complexes, although having taken many years to achieve their current character, may possibly be amenable to establishment, as a whole, in selected areas where industrial growth is desired. There will still be essential pre-conditions for success (e.g. an accessible market for the final products, adequate labour and managerial skills, etc.) and it may need to be added that industrial growth per se is by no means a panacea for the problems of underdeveloped areas.

Location leadership is not, of course, limited to manufacturing industries. The provision of major services, for example, especially those of a large port, also attracts industry, which proceeds to feed upon itself and grow. Centres of primary production, with coal as the outstanding example, may also become location leaders and give birth to major centres of industry.

Our thesis here, then, is that there are enterprises of large scale which comprise the fundamental industries and services in an industrial economy and are the pattern formers of the general distribution of industry and of the industrial population. Many smaller (and some not-so-small!) industries tend to follow the pattern set by the leaders, for their own optimum location occurs in proximity to them, ensuring the availability of materials or labour or markets or services, or all combined. The major industries of this type form the foundations of industrial agglomerations and have contributed by their presence to the growth of the major industrial regions of the world.

[1] Alexandersson, op. cit., p. 82. Contains many useful industrial studies
[2] An up-to-date introduction to this subject is C. Pratten and R. M. Deane, *The Economics of Large Scale Production in British Industry*, 1965
[3] E. A. G. Robinson, *The Structure of Competitive Industry*, 1953, p. 155
[4] A. J. Brown, *Introduction to the World Economy*, 1959, p. 127. Examples cited ibid., p. 124 ff.
[5] J. G. Stewart, Input-Output Table for the United Kingdom, *The Times Review of Industry*, December 1958 (London and Cambridge Bulletin)

9

INDUSTRY EXAMPLES I:

IRON AND STEEL

In the foregoing chapters we have attempted to examine the forces at play in determining the location of industrial activity. It would be idle to pretend that a detailed analysis of the locational requirements of any industry is possible in the space now remaining, but some extended illustration is nevertheless desirable within the covers of this book. Examples given in the text have often involved the simplification of actual cases, whereas few locations are simple in fact. We shall, therefore, attempt to examine a little more closely the locational requirements of three specific industries, and the present chapter is devoted entirely to the major industry of modern industrial civilisation—iron and steel.

This industry is one in which a large proportion of total productive capacity is normally concentrated at relatively few major centres of production. The map of blast furnace locations in the USA and Canada (Fig 2) shows clearly the concentration of capacity in the north-east and that within this region nine or ten districts dominate the industry. Steel-producing capacity shows on the whole a similar pattern, for there are considerable economies to be gained from the integration of all stages of production in one large plant. This coincidence of pattern can, however, be substantially modified by the use of scrap instead of pig iron in the steel furnace and by the use of the electric furnace, which mostly operates on scrap. Thus, while blast furnace capacity is now usually associated with steel production on the same site, some steel-making capacity exists where there are no blast furnaces. Nevertheless, the blast furnace locations shown on the map account also for about 85 per cent of total steel capacity in the USA.

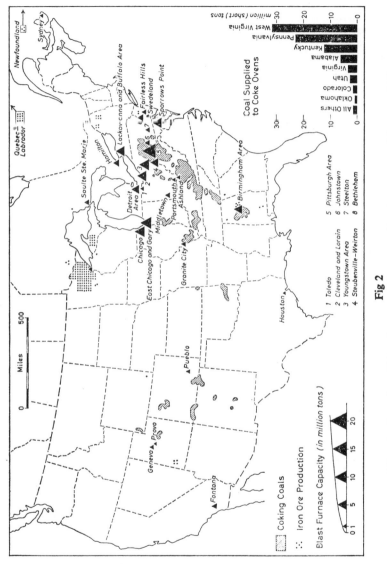

Fig 2

USA and Canada. Location of blast furnaces and sources of major raw materials, *circa* 1960
Source: American Iron and Steel Institute (blast furnace capacity) U.S. Minerals Year Book and Canada Year Book (iron ore production) U.S. Geological Society (coking coal areas)

This integration of processes normally means that maximum production economies are nowadays to be obtained only in a plant of very great size. The capacity of the separate units of production (blast furnaces, steel furnaces, rolling mills, etc.) is very large, and growing larger, and if each combination of units is to operate at maximum efficiency an annual production of two million or more tons may be required. Further relevant considerations in setting the *optimum* size of plant are the type of product and the size of the market. A works producing special steel products to meet a relatively small demand could operate efficiently with a capacity of under one million tons; a works so situated that it could provide an enormous market with a limited range of products may operate most economically at a much higher level— like the Sparrows Point, Maryland, works with its capacity of about 8 million tons. Such giants would be out of place in smaller economies like the UK, however, and here the optimum size, special cases apart, is probably now between 2 and 3 million tons.[1] With individual plants of such size, the number of significant locations is bound to be limited, and the correct location decision a matter of crucial importance.

Access to raw materials and to markets, and the structure of transfer costs, have been, in fact, the dominant elements in the location of this industry. Our most logical approach in this chapter, therefore, would be to follow the order of treatment adopted earlier in the book and outline some of the results of the operation of the influences described.

The traditional raw materials and fuels of the industry are coal (especially coking coal), iron ore, limestone, water[2] and scrap. Latterly, oil and electric power have been of increasing importance (oil, indeed, is now competing with coal at every stage of the steel-making process), but coal, ore and limestone supplies, all bulky and weight losing, still account for about three-quarters of the cost of the pig iron at the blast furnace, and access to them has always been a major concern in location. The map (Fig 2.) shows the centres of coking coal and iron ore production in USA and Canada at the present time, and we shall now discuss the role of both these vital materials.

Coal

The introduction of the use of coke in the blast furnace at various times in different countries between about 1750 and the late nineteenth century had the uniform result of strongly attracting the industry to sources of coking coal. The qualities demanded of metallurgical coke are important: few impurities to affect the quality of the iron; ability to withstand great pressure from material loaded above it in the furnace and still permit the free passage of circulating gases; a minimum of residual ash. Relatively few coal-producing areas possess coals of such quality, and this restricted the number of possible blast furnace locations in the early days of smelting with coke.

A decisive aspect of this 'pull' of coking coal was the large quantity used in producing a ton of pig iron. In the mid-eighteenth century some 8 to 10 tons were required. Technical advances, such as the Neilson hot blast (1828), reduced this requirement to about 4 tons by mid-nineteenth century and to about 2 tons by 1900. By 1938 it had been further reduced to about 1·8 tons in the UK and about 1·3 tons in USA.[3]

Meantime, similar economies were being achieved in other uses of coal by the industry. In the last two decades of the nineteenth century, following the steel-making inventions of Bessemer (1856), Siemens-Martin (1867) and Gilchrist-Thomas (1878), steel superseded wrought iron as the major product of the industry and this of itelf effected substantial economies in fuel. The Bessemer process, using cold air, was particularly economical. Later the integrated iron and steel works obtained further fuel economies by feeding the molten metal from blast furnaces direct to the steel furnaces, by using 'waste' gases from the furnaces and in other ways. So the total coal requirements per ton of steel produced fell from about 7 tons in 1850 to about 2 tons in the late 1930's.[4]

Over the years, therefore, the attractions of the coalfield for iron and steel production have diminished relative to other considerations. The occurrence of coking coals is no longer sufficient in itself to explain the existence of an iron and steel plant. But fuel and power requirements remain large (in the UK about 25 per cent of the total cost of producing a ton of steel[5]) and they still have to be weighed against other factors in deciding the optimum location in any given set of circumstances. The attraction of energy sources *per se* for new works is now seen most clearly in the locating of electric steel furnaces, which gain from a location near large supplies of cheap power, and in the increasing use of oil by the industry in oil deficit areas, such as western Europe, which increases the attractions of coastal locations. But many of the present centres of production (the Ruhr and the Pittsburgh-Youngstown area, for example) were developed when the 'pull' of coal was very great indeed, and coalfield locations consequently remain among the types most commonly found.

Iron ore

At the outset we should note that iron ores vary greatly in percentage of iron in the ore, in chemical composition, in the nature and quantity of impurities (phosphorus and sulphur, for example) as well as in the actual conditions of occurrence of the mineral body.[6] Such variations have been of no little importance in the location of iron and steel production and the timing of developments. The need, for example, to import non-phosphoric ores to produce pig iron for the new Acid Bessemer and Acid Open Hearth steel-making processses drew a considerable part of the UK industry to coastal locations from about 1860, while large reserves of accessible phosphoric ores remained unimportant until technical advance permitted their utilisation.

Access to ore has always been important in the location of iron production, but in the late eighteenth and early nineteenth centuries it happened in the UK that several areas possessing coals of coking quality also possessed iron ores in the coal measures themselves. This combination of advantages gave rise to important centres of production in the Black Country and elsewhere. Subsequently, when the coal measure ores declined, it became necessary to assess the different advantages of other areas.

Such special circumstances apart, the old maxim, 'iron ore moves to coal', was undoubtedly true through most of the nineteenth century, because of the very large quantities of coal used in production. As substantial fuel economies were achieved, however, it became less true, although, in fact, in many instances ore still moves towards coal. The areas marked 3 to 7 on Fig 2 are on the coal fields in eastern USA, while most of the other producing centres are nearer to coal than to ore. In Europe ore moves to coal in the most important producing area, the Ruhr, and in many other centres. The ores involved have usually been those of higher grade, but with the growth of beneficiation at the mine we can expect greater quantities of naturally low grade ore to move long distances to the furnace.

This continued tendency of ore to move to coal is in part the result of inertia, since the large-scale growth of the industry in coalfield locations in the nineteenth century is in itself a reason for their continuing prominence. The fact that coal *has* declined relative to ore in its locational pull from the late nineteenth century may be illustrated by the development of Lorraine and by the growth of the industry in Britain at coastal locations (for ore imports) and on the Jurassic orefields. Coastal locations, depending on rapidly growing seaborne ore imports, are of increasing importance also in the USA (cf. Fairless Hills and Sparrows Point), while a similar trend towards the use of more imported ore in Europe has recently played a part in the development of sites at Dunkirk, Bremen and elsewhere. Access to iron ore has, therefore, exerted a somewhat greater influence on location decisions in recent decades. It remains true, however, that ore has never played the decisive role in general location that coal once did.

The third of the raw materials for the blast furnace is limestone. This, however, is relatively abundant in nature, is used in smaller quantities than either coal or ore and is normally cheap at the blast furnace site. (See Table 11.) It therefore plays little, if any, part in normal location decisions and no further treatment is necessary here.

Material assembly

Because of the vast quantities of materials involved and the great loss of weight in processing, it might appear that the most advantageous location for the blast furnace would be at the point of minimum total movement of raw materials. So far as this is true, Birmingham, Alabama (see Fig 2) seems to be ideally placed in the United States. Only about 50 ton-miles of movement of coal, ore and flux are required to manufacture one ton of pig iron here, compared with about 500 ton-miles at Fontana, California, 600 at Pittsburgh and 1,000 at Gary, for example.[7] The United Kingdom would also seem to be at an advantage compared with other countries. Its small size and the disposition of resources are reflected in short hauls of ore to coal, coal to orefields or coal to imported ore at coastal locations. Burnham and Hoskins estimated that the average haul of raw materials to works in this country before the war was about 30 miles, compared with 150 miles in Germany, 160 in Belgium, 200 in France and 750 in USA.[8]

But length of haul is only one element in the movement of goods. Of equal or greater importance is the freight rate structure and the transport service, and Burnham and Hoskins found that the short-haul advantages of the United Kingdom had been (at least between 1870 and 1930) nullified by railway freight charges. Northamptonshire ores, for example, were trebled in cost by transport to Middlesbrough, while the cost of Lorraine ores in the

Ruhr was hardly more than doubled for a much longer journey.[9]
Thus distance of haul alone may be quite misleading as a guide
to assembly costs.

Other important considerations in this respect are the quality
and conditions of occurrence of the material transported. This is
reflected in the figures of raw materials consumption and assembly
costs presented in Table 11. The value of the situation at Birmingham, Alabama, is reduced by the 'relatively poor quality of its
iron ore and coking coal and by difficulties in mining them'.[10] By
using ore with an iron content of only some 36 per cent, the
Birmingham producers must haul greater quantities of ore to
produce a ton of metal than centres using, say, Mesabi ore with
50 per cent iron content. In addition the lower grade ore also needs
slightly more fuel and more flux per ton of iron produced. For
such reasons the assembly costs per ton of iron produced at
Birmingham, though low, are not as low as might at first sight be
expected, given the close proximity of raw materials. Further, the
relatively low assembly costs at Birmingham are not reflected in
equally low final costs of production. Ore mining is more expensive in the Birmingham area than at Mesabi and coalmining more
expensive than in northern Appalachia, raising the actual costs of
the materials at Birmingham. Add to this the fact that expensive
blast furnace capacity is rendered less productive when lower
grade materials are used, and we see clearly that assembly costs
are only one element in the final cost of the iron produced. In fact
it was estimated in 1950 that, despite transport costs very much
lower than those at Pittsburgh (Table 11), Birmingham pig iron
was about one dollar a ton dearer to produce.[11] In another instance the relatively low transport costs at Duluth compared with
Sparrows Point appear to be offset by the lower costs of raw
materials at the coastal site—a site which, moreover, has many
additional attractions. We must, therefore, keep haulage distance
and assembly costs in proper perspective in assessing their role in
location.

In ending this discussion of the 'pull' of coal and iron ore we
may note that new developments tend to decrease their attraction
still further. The practice of treating ore at the mine to reduce the
amount of waste to be transported is growing. Advances in the
techniques of beneficiation are permitting lean ores to be greatly
improved at, or near, the point of extraction, enabling them to be
economically transported over large distances. By 1962, for
example, about 85 per cent of iron ore shipped from mines in the

TABLE 11

CONSUMPTION AND COST OF RAW MATERIALS PER TON OF PIG IRON PRODUCED, USA 1950

Selected centres

	IRON ORE		COAL		LIMESTONE			Total cost of materials ($)	Total cost of transport ($)	Overall total ($)
	Consumption (lb)	Ore* cost ($) Transport cost ($)	Consumption (lb)	Coal cost ($) Transport cost ($)	Consumption (lb)	Lst. cost ($)	Transport cost ($)			
Birmingham	5,400	8·97 0·94	3,700	12·43 0·74	500	0·13	0·16	21·53	1·84	23·37
Chicago/Gary	4,032	4·46 4·55	2,350	7·14 5·02	1,000	0·24	0·37	11·84	9·94	21·78
Pittsburgh	4,032	4·29 8·23	2,485	7·16 0·78	1,000	0·24	0·68	11·69	9·69	21·38
Duluth	4,100	5·82 1·98	2,460	6·82 4·55	1,154	0·28	0·43	12·92	6·96	19·88
Sparrows Point	3,580	3·39 6·90	2,245	4·44 4·33	852	0·21	0·55	8·04	11·78	19·82
Fontana†	3,255	2·19 2·29	2,554	5·86 7·25	556	0·27	0·37	8·32	9·91	18·23
Geneva	3,780	3·41 3·42	2,880	6·12 3·28	918	0·23	0·40	9·76	7·14	16·90

Source: M. J. Barloon, Expansion of Blast Furnace Capacity, 1938–1952; *Business History Review* XXVIII (March 1954) No. 1

* Mining and Beneficiation

† Fontana, from C. Langdon White, 'Is the West making the grade in the Iron and Steel Industry?', *Stanford University Business Research Series*, No. 8, 1956

USA was being beneficiated, compared with about 25 per cent in 1950. Coal is also increasingly being treated at the mine, where washing, sizing and grading improve its transportability, while the attraction of high-grade coking coal is further diminished both by the practice of blending coals of poorer quality in the production of metallurgical coke and by technical advances which are decreasing the quantity of coke required in the production of pig iron. Shortly after the second world war a representative requirement of coke per ton of iron produced in the UK was about 23 cwt.; by 1964 this requirement had been reduced to about 14–15 cwt. Other advances in the efficiency of raw material utilisation also continue to be achieved, each with some kind of locational implication.

Scrap

Most pig iron from the blast furnace is now further processed into steel on the same site, and at this stage another element must be taken into account. The 'pull' of ore and coal on an integrated plant was substantially reduced by the increasing predominance of the Open Hearth Steel Furnace, which, unlike the Bessemer Converter, can use much scrap. On average about 50 per cent of the steel furnace charge in the UK is now scrap. The use of scrap has many advantages to offer. It contains a smaller proportion of impurities than pig iron and speeds the steel-making process. Moreover, it means that far less blast furnace capacity is required for the same steel production, thus saving heavy investment on blast furnaces. This in turn means that less coal and ore are required per ton of steel produced and this effects savings on associated investment such as for ore treating and coking plant.[12] The use of scrap, then, conserves both coal and ore, reduces their 'pull' and saves investment capital.

Access to outside scrap supplies, therefore, is now important to the steel industry and attracts it to established centres of industry. In other words, the heavy use of scrap strengthens the attractions of a market location for the steel industry and, consequently, often for blast furnace capacity, too. In the USA, the availability of large supplies of scrap in the north Atlantic coastal area and in the Chicago area has added to the other attractions of these expanding steel-producing centres. On the other hand, persistent shortage of locally arising scrap has contributed to the relative decline of the Pittsburgh area. 'Pittsburgh's productive capacity in steel] has always far exceeded its consumptive ability.' It was

developed to serve a national market. 'Consequently its local
market supplies a smaller proportion of scrap in terms of productive needs than do other areas.'[13] The price of scrap at Pittsburgh is accordingly invariably higher than in, for example,
Chicago, Sparrows Point and Detroit—an obvious disadvantage
to Pittsburgh. In the UK the availability of scrap supports steel
production, for example, in the Sheffield and west Midlands steel
works, where about three-quarters of the charge to steel furnaces
consists of scrap [14]

Market

Availability of scrap is only one of the advantages offered to the
industry by a market location and in general the market is becoming of increasing importance in the location decision as the attractions of coal and ore are lessened. It is not always easy, of course,
to distinguish between materials and markets in their effects on
location since, for example, developed coalfields are often both
materials and market areas. Nevertheless, the special 'pull' of the
market can be clearly seen in some instances. Pittsburgh, for
example, was relatively unimportant as an iron centre before
about 1850. Till then the main markets had been in the east, and
the main centres of production had also been there—in eastern
Pennsylvania. Pittsburgh, however, was better located for meeting the expanding Middle West market in the second half of the
nineteenth century and rapidly outgrew the eastern centres. It
endeavoured in the present century to perpetuate this supremacy
and to monopolise the national market by the basing point price
system, but the great development of markets for steel yet further
west (for agricultural equipment, food processing plant and railway materials) converted Chicago into a very favourable location.
This area had relatively high material assembly costs (as it still
has, see Table 11), but the advantages of an accessible expanding
market ensured the continuous growth of the industry, despite
Pittsburgh Plus. The growth of the market in the south, and in
more recent years in the west also, helps to explain the attractions
of these areas to iron and steel production.

The attractions of a location near a large market may be greatly
enhanced by freight-charging practices. Freight charges on steel
products are generally higher, sometimes very much higher, than
on raw materials. Thus, in USA, although the weight of the finished
product is much less than that of the raw materials required to
produce it, the cost of moving the product forms about 53 per

cent of total transport costs[15] and this despite a fairly close association with the market in many instances.

The importance of the market is further illustrated by the fact that inadequacy of market demand restricts the growth of the industry in many centres that would seem to be favourably endowed for iron and steel production. Kimberley, British Columbia, for example, is a location with considerable advantages for the assembly of raw materials,[16] but, though it could serve markets both in the Vancouver area and in Alberta, the total demand would still be insufficient to justify the large investment needed. The lack of a market of adequate size also handicaps New England in establishing a modern integrated works.[17] The effects of a poor location relative to markets can also be seen in established plants. The works at Duluth, Minnesota, and Sydney, Nova Scotia, are good examples, and they have signally failed to share in the recent general expansion of capacity in North America.[18]

To summarise the salient considerations in this respect, therefore, we must recall (a) the great advances that have been and are being made in reducing the quantities and the assembled costs of the coal and ore required per ton of finished steel, (b) that large quantities of purchased scrap are used in steel production and (c) the fact that transport rates on finished steel are higher than on raw materials. Given such conditions, it is apparent that the strongest locational pull is that of an established market (where it is of sufficient size), even though the pull of the market is not yet completely dominant.[19]

We must now examine the other influences at work. Although normally of relatively minor importance in this transport-oriented industry, they play a part in confirming existing locations, in balancing a marginal decision or in preventing development in an otherwise attractive situation.

Factors of production

The influence of the factors of production on iron and steel location is nowadays small in advanced industrial communities, although it has been of great importance in the past. In less developed areas their influence is still important.

The labour situation in USA is fairly representative of that in most industrialised countries. 'Though labour costs may be as high as 25 per cent of the total cost of the finished [steel] product, they are unimportant in the location pattern, because regional differences in labour costs per unit of output are minor today and are being rapidly eliminated by unionisation and training.'[20] It was not always so, and the recent history of Birmingham, Alabama, is illuminating.

In 1928 it was recorded as having the cheapest labour in the country.[21] Before the second world war these low wage rates helped to diminish the costs of mining coal and ore under relatively difficult physical conditions and, with the low assembly costs to which we have already referred, Birmingham was agreed to be the lowest cost producer of pig iron in the country. This advantage in the production of pig iron carried over into its production of steel ingots.[22] Birmingham, however, was denied more rapid expansion by the operation of the basing point pricing system (Chapter 2) and by the fact that the more important resources, plant and equipment in the Birmingham area were owned by the U.S. Steel Corporation, which had a direct interest in preserving the dominant position of the Pittsburgh area.[23] If Birmingham's prospects had depended solely on its labour and other cost advantages, the area would undoubtedly have developed much more, even though its local market was small. Since the war, however, unionisation of mineworkers and steelworkers and the migration of southern workers to the north and west have virtually eliminated the south's wage advantage.[24] The increased cost of mining coal and ore now outweighs Birmingham's lower assembly cost (see Table 11). Labour cost differentials have not entirely disappeared, but are small compared with other cost differentials, and their influence on location is now negligible.

Labour problems are more critical in under-developed countries and, as we saw in Chapter 4, embrace difficulties of both quality and availability.[25] Though labour may be plentiful and seriously under-employed, it may not be available at the place of production and has no skill or tradition of industrial employment. The assembly of a labour force and the provision of their housing and other needs raise initial capital requirements greatly. Though wages are low, labour costs tend to be high, and are further inflated by the need to attract skilled foreign technicians by high salaries. These disadvantages are surmountable, but they are handicaps and they do slow down the development of the industry. An example from India may be used to illustrate.

The Tata Iron and Steel Company's works at Jamshedpur was established in 1911. The location was admirable for raw material supplies and pig iron was produced at extremely low cost.[26]

F

Finished steel, however, has not been cheap, chiefly because labour and management were less efficient in the more exacting task of steel making,[27] and labour costs per ton of steel were high. But this location has now experienced half a century of industrial development and its present generation of industrial workers contains many native workers with technical and managerial skills. Nevertheless, although real wages are much lower than in Europe labour costs remain higher, because labour in general remains less efficient, and larger numbers have to be employed.[28]

The availability and costs of higher supervisory, managerial and entrepreneurial skills are also not usually important elements in iron and steel location in advanced industrial countries. Their significance should not, however, be underrated. The lack of progressive management in the UK between 1870 and 1930 was considered by Burnham and Hoskins to be one significant factor in the rapid relative decline of the UK as a world iron and steel producer. (In 1870 the UK produced about half the world's pig iron, in 1930 about 8 per cent.) Managerial posts at that time were usually passed from father to son, and management felt unhealthily secure.[29] This made for conservatism, hesitancy and opposition to change, while inadequate management was reflected in the incompetence of other supervisory personnel. 'There is, in fact, good evidence to believe that the British iron and steel industry would not have declined relatively so far or so fast . . . had the men at the head possessed greater vision and a bolder and more energetic capacity for organisation, direction and administration.'[30] The location of the industry as between different countries is therefore affected by the abilities or shortcomings of managers and executives. At the present time the paucity of trained native executive and managerial ability is a major difficulty in the establishment of the industry in under-developed areas.

The capital required to build a modern iron and steel works is tremendously large—up to £150 million for an integrated works of only medium size—and the availability of the necessary finance may affect the location decision. Within the national boundaries of advanced countries investment capital is, as we have seen, quite mobile and, on the surface at least, would seem to have little influence on actual location at the present time. But sufficient private investment capital is not always available and governments often provide large loans for development purposes. In supplying such a loan, the government may well demand a voice in the location decision. One thing, however, is certain: the large capital requirements ensure that the greatest care is taken in selecting the location for new capacity.

Another important consequence of the very high initial capital requirements for a new integrated plant is that the industry is relatively reluctant to develop completely new sites. It has been estimated, for the UK, that a completely new steel plant on a new site is about three times as expensive as the same capacity added to an existing plant.[31] An estimate for USA suggests that the cost per ingot ton of annual capacity added to an existing plant would be only a quarter to a half of that on a 'greenfield site'.[32] Existing locations are therefore as far as possible developed (or re-developed) when new capacity is required. This principle guided most of the new developments in Europe, and in USA, for the first twelve years or so after the war, being aided in its application by technical advances which permitted greatly increased output from existing, or remodelled, plant. 'Despite the almost constant excess of demand for steel over supply since the war, there is not an integrated steel works in operation today [1957] in the European Coal and Steel Community which has been built since 1945 on a greenfield site.'[33] Elsewhere, greenfield sites were also the exception in countries possessing well-established iron and steel industries, although the exceptions (as, for example, at Fairless Hills, USA) were important. The heavy capital investment in existing plant and the high capital cost of new site development thus make for inertia in this industry. Naturally there is a limit to the additions in productive capacity that can be made to works in existing locations, while technological developments and changing patterns of materials supply and consumer demand may so alter the requirements of desirable location that, when new capacity is required, it will be provided on a greenfield site, even, perhaps, in a completely new location. This appears to have been the general situation since about 1957.[34] Since that time, while valuable and economical investment has continued to be made in many existing plants, large new locations have been developed, as, for example, in Europe at Newport and Dunkirk.

Whenever large quantities of capital for long-term investment are not readily available, progress in the iron and steel industry is not possible. To illustrate again from UK experience between 1870 and 1930, the urgent need for replacement equipment and for the adoption of new methods was not matched by the supply of the necessary investment capital. Although not stressing the part this played in the relative decline of the British industry, Burnham and Hoskins describe it as 'a relative weakness'.[35]

In the under-developed countries of the world today, however, the scarcity of investment capital is not a relative weakness but an 'overwhelming difficulty'.[36] Initial capital requirements are generally greater than for providing the same capacity in a developed area. The plant and equipment must be imported and a great deal of ancillary development is often essential to provide access to materials and markets, accommodation for labour and necessary services for both the plant and its personnel (e.g. electricity, water, waste disposal). In India a rapid increase in industrial output after Independence was greatly handicapped by an acute shortage of steel. The Planning Commission in its 1951 report, however, found that, although the country was well endowed with the essential raw materials, a significant expansion of steel capacity was ruled out by financial obstacles.[37] In the end a remedy was found in negotiating agreements between the Indian government and other governments (Western Germany, Russia and the UK) which enabled an iron and steel development programme to be partially financed by long-term loans from those countries.

Government

This example of government action in India brings us now to consider the role of governments generally in the location of this industry. The world distribution of the industry has been affected by the desire of governments to establish domestic iron and steel industries. This is well exemplified in Japan. The main period of development began in 1896, when the government established the Imperial Steel Works at Yawata, and it was not until the first world war that there were any real private interests in steel production. The next important period of development was between 1933 and 1943, when steel production grew from c. $2\frac{1}{2}$ to almost 8 million tons. This was 'not the result of haphazard developments by private enterprise but of methodical planning by the Japanese government'.[38] This government direction was considered essential because of the poor indigenous resources. The main centres, dependent essentially on imported raw materials, were naturally located at tidewater. The Japanese government also undertook the development of the Manchurian iron and steel industry in the 1930's and early 1940's, treating Manchuria 'as an extension of the homeland'.[39]

Government intervention in the location of iron and steel

capacity has sometimes been on social or 'socio-economic' grounds. In all communist states, of course, location is a matter of government decision; and the choice of location for the Nowa Huta plant in Poland is interesting in this context because it was not based on raw material or market access but 'rather the urgent need to create employment in the Krakow area'.[40] In southern Italy the large new plant at Taranto is part of the government programme for developing industry in the region, while in the UK government intervention has also been based on grounds of unemployment. The case of Ebbw Vale in the 1930's was mentioned in Chapter 6. More recently (late 1958), after some eighteen months of debate, the Prime Minister announced the Cabinet decision that new strip mill capacity planned by Richard Thomas and Baldwin for a greenfield site near Newport, Monmouthshire, would in fact be split between that firm at that site and Colville's at Ravenscraig, Lanarkshire. 'If the choice had been made on technical grounds alone there is no doubt that only one strip mill would have been built . . . and at Newport. The Colville's project is the result of political pressure from Scotland.'[41] The government's power is derived both from its control of the issue of Industrial Development Certificates and from the fact that much of the necessary initial capital will be in the form of government loans.

Governments also protect native iron and steel industries against competition in order to allow them to become firmly established, or in order to retain a sufficient home market or to nurse them through difficult periods. Such measures affect the world distribution of the industry. In the UK, for example, a high protective tariff was applied in the 1930's, behind which equipment, techniques and organisation were to be improved. The British Iron and Steel Federation was created 'to foster re-organisation schemes' and was 'formally subject to the supervision of the Import Duties Advisory Committee'.[42] Overseas, the Canadian industry generally has been protected against American and European competitors by import duties, but the Canadian government has been particularly concerned for the Sydney, Nova Scotia, plant. This operates at a substantial relative disadvantage. It is close to coal, but not good coking varieties; it is well placed to receive Newfoundland ore, but this is high in phosphorus and silica and compares unfavourably with Mesabi ore; local scrap is insufficient to meet requirements; it is far removed from the major market areas. But, with government help, it still produces about

16 per cent of total pig iron and 14 per cent of total steel output in Canada.[43] Examples could be multiplied; there are few countries in which the iron and steel industry is without some form of government assistance.

The impact of national strategy on location was illustrated in Chapter 6 from Germany (Salzgitter) and USA (Geneva and Fontana). We have also noted elsewhere that direct government intervention is now generally regarded as essential in the establishment of iron and steel industries in under-developed areas. In India, for example, the steel industry is regarded officially as one for whose further development 'the State is responsible, except to the extent that the co-operation of private enterprise is from time to time considered necessary'.[44]

In short, governments everywhere display a serious interest in the fortunes of their iron and steel industries and play a sometimes decisive role in the location of the industry both internationally and regionally.

Other influences

Among other features of importance in explaining existing locations *inertia* has particular significance in this industry. Heavy investment in fixed plant; the proximity of industries serving, or being served by, the established plant; the scrap supplies arising in established areas; the labour situation; the established trade connections and reputations; the substantial economies achieved by expanding capacity at existing sites when new capacity is needed—these are among the features that give inertia its strength in this industry. The key to the understanding of many locations lies in the conditions of production, techniques, forms and methods of transport, freight charging and steel pricing practices in the past.

Pittsburgh is an admirable example of inertia and, though the location now suffers from certain comparative disadvantages, it retains a very large share of national capacity. (See Fig 2.) Its prominence, then, has to be explained by reference to past conditions of production, and pricing and marketing. In our own country Sheffield is a good example of inertia. It produces about two-thirds of UK alloy steel, nearly all its high-speed steel and a large proportion of other high value products.[45] This large concentration of special steel manufacture is largely attributable to the history of the area in steel making and working.

But the mere existence of the industry at some time in a given location is no guarantee of its continuance there. 'Under conditions of free competition the fixed investment in plant located in the past under different conditions can offset only for a limited period superior natural advantages of other locations.'[46] The features sustaining the leading position of some older centres are often more dynamic than the term 'inertia' suggests. These locations still offer positive productive advantages of the type mentioned above, but in addition they may remain of outstanding importance because they are centres of research and innovation. Sheffield, for example, saw the birth, or first application, of such fundamental processes as those developed by Huntsman and Bessemer. More recently it pioneered a multitude of special alloys, and there is solid evidence at the present time that its inventiveness is far from finished. The eminence of such centres, then, is not purely an immobile thing based only on past traditions and investment. They are energetic centres, not merely alive but progressive. Locations that do not retain such positive advantages do not remain significant merely because of their past histories.

Among the most important influences causing location requirements to change over time is *technological advance*. The invention of the Basic Process, for example, in 1878 made possible the use of pig iron made from phosphoric ores in steel production, and this permitted the growth of the steel industry in Lorraine. The results of advances in efficiency of use of coal and ore have already been indicated, and the process continues, the growing practice of charging the blast furnaces with sintered ore making one of the most important contributions to economy in the use of both ore and coke in recent years. Other new techniques, widely adopted recently, have served greatly to increase the capacity of individual plants. Thus the average output per blast furnace in the UK rose by about 50 per cent between 1955 and 1962, and comparable advances have been made in steel production. The use of oxygen has had a particularly beneficial effect on efficiency and economy in recent years, while the new methods of continuous casting of steel hold similar promise.[47] Such advances often help to increase the importance, or to maintain the status, of existing locations to which they can be applied.

Actual *site requirements* for a modern integrated works are important. Extensive areas of level and cheap land are required—the new Abbey-Margam works in south Wales, for example, covers about four square miles. In addition to space for the productive plant itself, the site needs room for elaborate internal communications systems, raw material stocks, waste disposal and, desirably, for future expansion. Such requirements are not easily met, while the need for external transport facilities and enormous water supplies further limits the number of possible sites. Existing centres developed on what have since proved restricted sites are at a serious disadvantage. One of the marked drawbacks at Pittsburgh is the congestion and lack of room for expansion and redevelopment on the narrow valley floors. By contrast, favourable site conditions along the Great Lake shores, especially around Chicago–Gary, have given further opportunity for expansion. In the UK Ebbw Vale is an example of a restricted site not well suited to a modern works. The narrow valley floors not only leave little room for expansion but also make the attainment of efficient lay-out almost impossible. Thus its share of total UK steel output has fallen since the war and the plant is unable to meet the expanding needs of the local strip mill. Large quantities of steel slab have to be brought from elsewhere at considerable expense and the product is moved out of the area again after rolling.

The effect of *local activities* may be illustrated by reference to Hamilton (Ontario) and Duluth (Minnesota). At Hamilton, the first blast furnace was built in 1895 'mainly because of tax concessions offered the company by the city'.[48] A location was being sought in this general area and the local concession was probably the decisive feature. Hamilton is now the largest producer in Canada. The Duluth location on the other hand was not the result of an attractive offer by local interests, but was apparently developed by the company in order to avoid a threatened State tax on ore exports from Minnesota.[49] The industry here, however, has not flourished.

Finally we must consider *water supply*, for the requirements of this industry are tremendous (see Chapter 7), although much is re-used. Consumption varies, however, with conditions of supply. The Chicago–Gary area, for example, is among the largest users of water per ton of steel produced, for location alongside Lake Michigan makes water supply a cheap and easy matter. In fact the cost of water there has been estimated at about 0·2 cents per thousand gallons.[50] By contrast, at Fontana, California, water supply is difficult. Kaiser originally wanted a site on tidewater at Los Angeles, but a government loan was made conditional on a location fifty miles inland. The result is that the cost of water is about ten times that at Chicago, but the consumption per ton of steel is the lowest in the country. The Pittsburgh–Youngstown area is intermediate between Fontana and Chicago in its water situation, and certain difficulties are reflected in costs which, at Youngstown, are about five times the Chicago figure.

'When once the problems of assembling coking coal, iron ore and limestone at the blast furnace and of supplying markets with steel have been solved, the availability of a huge supply of water of good quality and at reasonable cost becomes a major location factor. . . Because water is used in such large quantities, It is not practicable to transport it, as is the case with iron ore and coal.'[51]

This means that the role of water in the location decision is normally to help fix the precise site within an area considered to be favourable from other points of view. Where water supply presents some difficulty, its influence becomes more rigorous, as in the siting of the Geneva (Utah) plant and the Tata works at Jamshedpur;[52] and as the iron and steel industry expands in the less well watered countries of the world, water supply could well become important in the selection of location, or situation, as well as site.

Thus, while coal and fuels, iron ore and markets have been 'the three major regional factors . . . determining the geographical patterns of iron and steel production',[53] many other circumstances have influenced the actual choice of location or have caused the nature of the optimum location to change over the years. The ideal location probably does not exist. Indeed, if it did exist at any point of time, it would not remain the 'ideal' for long, given the continuous technical advance. The best possible location in this, as in any other, industry is a matter of compromise and depends on the particular conditions at the time and place concerned—physical, technical, economic, social and political.

---

[1] C. Pratten and R. M. Dean, *The Economics of Large Scale Production in British Industry* (1965), Chap 4

[2] Water is dealt with separately at the end of this section

[3] W. Isard, 'Some Location Factors in the Iron and Steel Industry since the early 19th century', *Journal of Political Economy*, vol. LVI, 1948

[4] Ibid.

[5] Pratten and Dean, op. cit., p. 79.

[6] A valuable introduction to a study of iron ores, and of the industry in general, will be found in this same series: *The Geography of Iron and Steel*, by

N. J. G. Pounds, 1959. It may be useful to note here, too, that the quality of iron ore will affect the type and design of equipment, the quantities of coke required, etc., and thus affect the costs of smelting.

[7] J. E. Brush, 'The Iron and Steel Industry of India', *Geographical Review*, 1952, p. 52

[8] T. H. Burnham and G. O. Hoskins, *Iron and Steel in Britain 1870–1930*, 1943, p. 104

[9] Ibid., p. 112

[10] G. W. Stocking, *Basing Point Pricing and Regional Development*, 1954, p. 80

[11] E. C. Wright, quoted in Stocking, op. cit., p. 150

[12] See N. J. G. Pounds, 'World Production and Use of Steel Scrap', *Economic Geography*, 1959

[13] Isard, op. cit., p. 215

[14] *Steel Review*, no. 11, 1958, p. 33

[15] A. Rodgers, 'Industrial Inertia, a major factor in the Location of the Steel Industry in the United States', *Geographical Review*, 1952

[16] D. Kerr, 'The Geography of the Canadian Iron and Steel Industry', *Economic Geography*, 1959

[17] W. Isard and J. H. Cumberland, 'New England as a Possible Location for an Integrated Iron and Steel Works', *Economic Geography*, 1950

[18] C. Langdon White and G. Primmer, 'The Iron and Steel Industry of Duluth: a Study in Locational Maladjustment', *Geographical Review*, 1937; and Kerr, op. cit.

[19] Isard and Cumberland, op. cit., p. 247

[20] Rodgers, op. cit., p. 57. Pratten and Dean (op. cit., p. 79) estimate that 'wages, salaries and national insurance' account for about 22 per cent of total costs in an integrated UK steel works in 1964

[21] C. Langdon White, 'Iron and Steel Industry of the Birmingham (Alabama) District', *Economic Geography*, 1928

[22] Stocking, op. cit., pp. 83–4 and Table 8

[23] See Stocking, op. cit.

[24] Ibid., p. 150

[25] For a detailed study of labour and other problems in such areas see Alan B. Mountjoy, *Industrialisation and Under-developed Countries* (Hutchinson Univ. Lib. Series), 1963

[26] British Iron and Steel Federation, *The Indian Steel Industry*, 1955

[27] Brush, op. cit.

[28] B.I.S.F., *The Indian Steel Industry*, p. 8

[29] Burnham and Hoskins, op. cit., p. 248

[30] Ibid., p. 271

[31] *Economist*, 8 June 1957, p. 890. A striking example can be seen in the proposal (1965) to increase capacity at the Newport steel works from 1·4 to 2 million tons. The existing capacity on this greenfield site cost £140 million. The addition of 0·6 million tons to this capacity is estimated to require a further £10 million only. In other words, the existing capacity can be raised by more than 40 per cent with an investment amounting to well under 10 per cent of the original requirement. It ought to be added, however, that some of the capacity originally installed was in excess of the immediate need.

[32] B.I.S.F., *Steel Review, no. 11*, 1958, p. 32

[33] B.I.S.F., *Steel Review, no. 5*, 1957, p. 53

[34] Ibid., p. 54

[35] Op. cit., chapters II and VIII

[36] B.I.S.F., *The Indian Steel Industry*

[37] Ibid., p. 3

[38] M. Erselcuk, 'Iron and Steel Industry of Japan', *Economic Geography*, 1947, p. 106

[39] A. Rodgers, 'The Manchurian Iron and Steel Industry', *Geographical Review*, 1940, p. 41

[40] N. J. G. Pounds, 'Nowa Huta. A New Polish Iron and Steel Plant', *Geography*, 1958, p. 54

[41] *The Times Review of Industry*, December 1958

[42] G. C. Allen, *British Industries and their Organization*, 3rd ed., p. 112

[43] Kerr, op. cit., p. 163

[44] B.I.S.F., *Indian Steel Industry*, op. cit., p. 5

[45] B.I.S.F., *Steel Review, no. 11*, 1958, p. 35

[46] L. Hartshorne, 'Location Factors in the Iron and Steel Industry', *Economic Geography*, 1928

[47] See the Iron and Steel Institute Special Report No. 75, *Productivity in the Iron and Steel Industry*, 1962; also Sir A. McCance, 'The Steel Industry Today and Tomorrow', *Journal of the Royal Society of Arts*, July 1961; and British Iron and Steel Federation, *Research in the U.K. Steel Industry*, 1964

[48] Kerr, op. cit., p. 154

[49] White and Primmer, op. cit.

[50] Langdon White, 'Water—neglected factor in the Geographical Literature of Iron and Steel', *Geographical Review*, 1957. This section is based largely on this article

[51] Ibid., p. 468

[52] Brush, op. cit., p. 44

[53] Isard, op. cit., p. 203, fn. 4

INDUSTRY EXAMPLES II:

MOTOR VEHICLE MANUFACTURE;

OIL REFINING

Motor vehicle manufacture

The motor vehicle industry has risen swiftly in the present century to a position of outstanding importance in the economies of a few highly industrialised countries, and it possesses several distinctive features. Almost 60 per cent of total world production takes place in one country, the USA. The industry is dominated, both in USA and elsewhere, by a few firms producing on enormous scale. It has had, too, a very strong tendency towards geographical concentration, although that tendency is now beginning to weaken somewhat. Finally, its fortunes, far more than in most industries, have extremely far-reaching economic and social ramifications.

Table 10 indicated some aspects of the importance of the industry in USA. In addition its fortunes affect the makers of iron and steel, non-ferrous metal products, machinery and tools, electrical products, springs, bolts, nuts, paint, rubber, leather and plastic—to name but a few. There was more than a grain of truth in the statement attributed to an official of a leading firm: 'What's good for General Motors is good for the country.' In the UK we have seen (Chap. 8) that in a single year the motor industry purchased goods to the value of more than £200 million from no fewer than 24 out of a total of 38 industrial groups. Direct employment in motor manufacturing now amounts to some 483,000 and, if employment in other industries directly attributable to the motor industry's requirements is taken into account, a million or more people must depend on the industry for their livelihood.[1] The economic implications are obvious, but this high degree of dependence on outside industries also has locational implications for the motor vehicle industry.

(a) Early development and location

The motor industry has been called a 'typically American industry', and there is some truth in this. Though initially behind Europe in the development of the petrol engine, the Americans made a major contribution by developing techniques of production that converted a limited market for an expensive product into a mass market for a mass-produced vehicle. The methods developed by H. Ford and others in the USA not only revolutionised car manufacture but had profound repercussions throughout industry. We may briefly trace developments, then, through American experience.

The manufacture of automobiles in the USA was at first chiefly done by existing firms, approaching motor vehicle production from their existing interest. Thus bicycle manufacturers in Hartford (Connecticut), Indianapolis, Cleveland, Toledo and elsewhere undertook automobile construction as a sideline from the 1890's. The makers of horse-drawn carriages and wagons in such cities as Terre Haute, South Bend, St Louis, Flint and Detroit also branched out into automobile manufacture in the early days of the present century. Some engineering firms, producers of mechanical equipment and other manufacturers, also provided recruits to the early industry. This kind of 'migration' into car production was natural and important. Such industries were already using steel and iron, brass parts, springs, wheels, axles, paints, gears and other materials and components that the motor vehicle required. Further, the parent firm provided the initial capital, plant and production facilities, plus technically skilled personnel and entrepreneurs 'who were accustomed to think in terms of producing vehicles in large quantity'.[2] Outside USA the story was much the same in kind, but different in scale. In Coventry, for example, many firms found their way into car manufacture via an earlier interest in cycles.

Thus at the beginning of the century in USA automobile manufacturing was predominantly a sideline to other industrial operations. It was 'still minute in stature [and] it was also inferior in technology to contemporary European development'.[3] During the following ten years, however, it grew to independent status, the sideline becoming the main operation and many newcomers entering the field. Entry was easy at this stage, since the firms were simply assemblers, on a relatively small scale, of materials and components bought in. Initial capital requirements were small and the risks involved were spread from the assembling firm over many suppliers, who in turn were not wholly committed at this stage to the vehicle industry. The assembly requirements were naturally reflected in location, proximity to component supplies being very desirable. But this was not the only element in success, and a quotation from E. A. G. Robinson is particularly apt for this stage of development. 'The location of industry is . . . the consequence also of a certain competitive selection. Motor firms spring up like grass after Indian rains; they die almost as quickly. They survive only if they have wisely chosen their methods, their designs and their location.'[4]

The main centres of automobile production that emerged in the first years of the century were in New England and the Middle West.[5] By 1910, however, the New England challenge for supremacy had virtually disappeared, largely because the producers had not 'wisely chosen their design'. They had mainly concentrated on steam-driven and electric automobiles which were soon proved inferior to the internal combustion engine, favoured by most midwest undertakings. Most of the hundreds of new entrants to the industry produced petrol-driven vehicles and tended to concentrate in lower Michigan and the adjacent portions of Ohio and Indiana, which by 1910 had attracted the bulk of the industry.[6] Detroit in particular, with much vigorous development, came to be the chief centre, attracting yet more capital, more technical skill and more entrepreneurial ability.

It was at Detroit in 1908 that Ford introduced his new assembly line technique, and the era of modern mass production began. Others followed suit and production in USA rose from c. 65,000 vehicles in 1908 to c. 1,900,000 in 1917. The first world war stimulated the industry in the USA (in Europe it had the opposite effect), and in 1920 production reached 2·2 million vehicles and rose swiftly to an inter-war peak of 5·3 million in 1929.[7]

One important effect of the new methods was to make entry into the industry much more difficult. Very large initial capital investment and a very high degree of technical and administrative skill were now required. Substantial economies could be achieved by the large firm, producing and marketing on a very large scale. Thus, while the total output of vehicles rose rapidly, the number of manufacturers declined sharply. In 1914 there were about 300 motor vehicle firms;[8] in 1923, 108; and in 1927, 44, of which three

(General Motors, Ford and Chrysler) produced about 75 per cent of all cars made. The great depression of the 1930's hit smaller firms severely. The big firms, though not unscathed, weathered the storm more effectively, and by 1939 the Big Three accounted for 90 per cent of total output.[9]

Productive capacity had become highly concentrated geographically in the Detroit region, and remains so to the present time

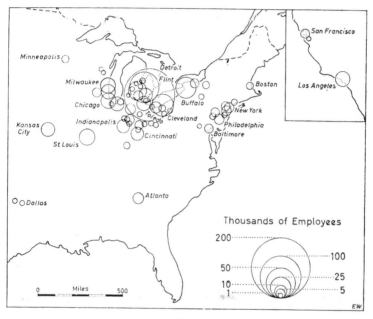

Fig 3

USA employment in the motor vehicle and equipment industry, 1962
(For standard metropolitan areas and counties employing 1,000 or more
in this industry)

Source: USA Department of Commerce. County Business Patterns. 1962

(see Fig 3). In 1962 some two-thirds of all workers in motor vehicle and parts manufacturing in the USA were in Michigan, Ohio and Indiana. Michigan itself had 44 per cent, and the Detroit Metropolitan Area alone just over 25 per cent. The degree of concentration has tended to decrease in recent years (e.g. in 1954 the three-state proportion was 70 per cent) but it nevertheless remains a remarkable geographical phenomenon.

This short retrospect implies that three main groups of features have been of particular importance in location—the economies of large-scale production, the necessity for access to supplies and to the market, and the role of the factors of production. These and other influences may now be discussed separately.

(b) Scale

From the time of Ford's introduction of the moving assembly line, using standardised components to produce large numbers of identical vehicles, and replacing skilled workers by semi-skilled operatives, each performing a limited task, the advantage in the production of cars has lain with the firm that could meet the high initial capital costs and organise the production and marketing of the product effectively. With hundreds of separate operations to be dovetailed smoothly, with all the varied units of production to be kept operating so as to ensure lowest total costs per unit, and with the need to develop and maintain a mass market, the optimum scale of production became very large.

The production of a motor vehicle involves six main groups of operation: the design and development of the vehicle; purchasing materials and components; making the body; making the engine, gearbox, axles, suspension and other components; assembling body and components; distributing selling, and servicing the finished vehicle.[10] The chief economies of scale are obtained in the third and fourth operations, where labour-saving investment, and an increase in the number of standardised parts used in all vehicles, bring much lower costs. When competing firms produce several vehicle designs, there is a great deal of associated 'waste' in making several bodies, engines, gearboxes and so on. A merger into one large firm permits economical rationalisation. Two or three engine and gearbox units, for example, can serve *all* the models produced. Bodies can be simple variations on a single basic design, which brings enormous economies. For example, dies for making five variations on a single design for British Motor Corporation vehicles cost £1½ million, while the cost of dies for five separate bodies would have been £5 million.[11] Economies of scale in these operations stimulate economies in the other operations—e.g. in design and development and in outside purchasing. Significantly, the economies of scale give less return at the assembly stage. A plant to assemble 4,000 units per week may cost little less than two plants for 2,000 a week.[12] This means that, at least from the investment point of view, the assembly stage can be separated among several smaller plants rather than concentrated in one large plant. The geographical dispersal of the assembly stage is, therefore, possible and may offer its own economies. This is referred to again.

Economies in the actual production process, however, are not the only reasons for large-scale operation and for the domination of the industry by a few giant organisations. The distribution and selling is also a major task, and certain economies of scale are ordained, for example, in advertising costs, show-room costs and so on. The small or medium-sized firms in this industry certainly face great marketing problems, which decrease their chances of survival in present-day conditions.

It is clear, then, that this is an industry in which the large-scale producer has overwhelming advantages. In the USA in 1963 three firms accounted for 92 per cent of total output—and two of these alone for 79 per cent. In the UK up to 1913 there had been 198 different makes of car marketed, of which fewer than half still remained in production. In 1922 there were 96 firms; in 1939, 33 firms.[13] In the latter year the three leading UK firms produced about two-thirds of the total output,[14] which was, however, only about one-tenth of that of USA. Up to this time, therefore, the British industry was less concentrated (functionally) than in the USA. In many ways the UK industry was behind the times and produced a large number of different vehicles, while the process of component standardisation was relatively little advanced. Mass-production methods were not adopted by the large producers here until about the mid 1920's. Morris Motors did not begin to use the moving assembly line until 1934.[15] Since 1945, however, the British industry has gone far towards adopting the American type of organisation.[16] Smaller firms have amalgamated, been absorbed by larger organisations, or have gone out of business altogether.[17] By 1963 four firms, the British Motor Corporation, Ford, Vauxhall and Rootes, accounted for about 90 per cent of total car production—the first two, indeed, accounting for more than 70 per cent, which leaves little enough room for the others. Apart from the 'Big Four' there are perhaps a dozen or so firms of some significance engaged in car manufacture, but few of these are concerned chiefly with car production. For most it is a sideline of greater or lesser importance. Most of these smaller producers, however, face considerably difficulty in making and selling their cars at a profit against competition

G

from the large corporations with their significant economies of scale.

Large-scale production is thus one of the most important features of the motor vehicle industry, and no understanding of its location can be achieved without bearing this in mind. Naturally, the securing of the economies of very large-scale assembly of hundreds of components is easiest if the functional concentration we have been describing is accompanied by geographical concentration, although there are important exceptions, especially at the final assembly stage. We have already stressed the extent of the geographical concentration in USA. In the UK the recognised geographical centre of the industry lies in the Midlands, a region which in 1964 accounted for 37 per cent of the national total of employment in this industry. Most of the remaining employment is also close at hand, especially in Oxford, Luton, Dagenham and south Lancashire. In fact approximately 85 per cent of the national total of employment in motor vehicle manufacture still occurs within a distance of 100 miles from Coventry, despite the governmental pressures for dispersal which are discussed below. Geographically the UK industry thus has a concentration just as marked as that in the United States. We may now attempt to assess some reasons why the concentrations grew where they did.

(c) Material and market access

The industry needs economic access to materials and components in enormous quantity, and to be so organised in their supply as to permit the smooth functioning of the very large plant. The motor vehicle is an assemblage of some thousands of separate parts, a significant proportion of which are bought-in from outside suppliers as finished or semi-finished components. Thus unlike the iron and steel industry this industry will have little direct relationship with natural resources, but will be intimately concerned with the location of developed manufacturing potential in a wide range of materials and products. Table 12 gives a broad approximation of its costs structure in the UK.

These figures illustrate the importance of purchased materials and components. Dynamos, starting motors, steering gear, castings, brake linings, propeller shafts and many other items are normally produced in specialist firms, which make them in large quantities and therefore more cheaply than the individual motor vehicle firm could. An important element in this type of specialisation is the standardisation of many of these components, the specialist firms producing only a limited range of types for all buyers. The extent of this reliance on outside firms seems, however, to be decreasing. In the USA, the practice of making parts and components within the firm has been growing for some time, and all the big firms control their own body manufacture. The same trend is evident in the UK; body-building firms have been

TABLE 12

APPROXIMATE COSTS STRUCTURE IN
UK MOTOR VEHICLE INDUSTRY

Purchased materials and components		58%
of which Sheet steel and pressings	*c.* 6·0	
Other iron and steel	*c.* 13·0	
Non-ferrous metals	*c.* 3·5	
Electrical equipment	*c.* 5·5	
Rubber	*c.* 3·5	
Bought-in components	*c.* 4·5	
Upholstery	*c.* 1·0	
Paint	*c.* 1·0	
Glass	*c.* 1·0	
Miscellaneous purchases	*c.* 18·5	
Wages, salaries and employees' benefits		19%
Other operating expenses		5%
Depreciation and replacement		5%
Net profit		6%
Taxes		7%
		100%

(Calculated from the *Economist*, 'Motors in the Boom', 22 October 1955)

acquired by the vehicle manufacturers and all are reaching out into the production of components.

This process of vertical integration, however, does not necessarily lead to the gathering together of the many stages of production at one very large site. In countries where the motor vehicle industry has been established for some time the main centres of manufacture of parts and components remain, irrespective of ownership, largely in areas where they initially grew. Now this initial growth was, as we saw in USA, out of certain pre-existing industries which broadened their interests into the field of automobile and component part manufacture. For newcomers to the field, access to materials and parts supplies was essential and became more important as the scale of operations grew. 'Once the manufacture of motor vehicles became a genuinely large-scale operation, requiring a constant flow of materials in enormous quantities, this factor [accessibility of materials] was bound to be decisive.'[18] With the early industry therefore dependent upon existing manufacture, an excellent combination of advantages occurred in the mid-west of USA. The supply of metal and other components was good, already serving the existing wagon, machinery and engineering industries, and many firms began to make parts for motor vehicles as a sideline. As the industry took hold here, more enterprises grew in and around such early centres as Toledo, Cleveland, Flint and Detroit to supply the growing industry with some of its many needs, and the concentration fed upon itself and grew still further.

In the UK 'the industry became concentrated in the district where American conditions found their closest parallel', i.e. the west Midlands. 'In the local brass, screw, nut and bolt, paint, pressed steel, tube, iron-foundry, leather, spring and plating trades, there was a multitude of small independent producers who could adapt themselves to the manufacture of motor parts.'[19] These conditions helped to give the west Midlands a lead that it has not yet relinquished, and practically all important motor vehicle manufacture in the country takes place within about one hundred miles of Birmingham and Coventry.

At the present time considerable economies can still be gained from the geographical concentration of plant supplying materials, components and sub-assemblies. In the USA the chief steel centres remain in the Middle West, and the leading automobile cities have established their own steel capacity. Access to steel strip, therefore, as well as to mechanical and electrical components, remains excellent here, and is especially important in the earlier stages of production. In UK the main suppliers of steel strip, at Margam, Ebbw Vale, Newport and Shotton, are close to the Midlands, while component manufacturers are almost entirely found in a rectangular area stretching from south Lancashire through the west Midlands to the London region. Thus, for access to materials and components the best location for the car industry in the UK remains in the same area.

Of equal importance in the growth and location of the industry has been access to a market, national or international, large

enough to absorb its output. The chief reason for the dominance
of USA in world motor vehicle production is the fact that the
American industry early tapped a mass market for cars, and that
America, with the highest standards of living in the world, remains
the largest market. *Within* that country access to the biggest potential internal market for cars helped to bring about the geographical
concentration that we have noted. 'The mid-west, with its sprawl-
ing land expanses and scattered trade centres, was more transport
conscious than was the East.'[20] In other words, more people were
interested in travelling longer distances, and in a shorter time,
than was possible by horse-drawn vehicle or bicycle. Subsequently,
when the market had become nation wide, the mid-west was placed
as well as, or better than, any other centre to serve it.

A further significant consequence of the assembly nature of this
industry is that the organisation of production can be grouped
in three broad divisions. Each of these may be economically
located apart from the others if the economies gained by such
physical separation outweigh the normal economies of agglomeration. The divisions are (i) the manufacture of individual parts
(e.g. pistons, piston rings, engine blocks, valves, springs, collets,
etc.); (ii) the assembly of these separate parts into units or 'sub-
assemblies' (in this case the engine unit); (iii) the final assembly of
the whole vehicle. With the technical maturing of the industry in
the past two decades, and the wider distribution of markets to
which many thousands of vehicles have to be transported, the
attractions of a market location have proved very great for the
final assembly stage.

We have seen that in capital cost it is not much more economic
to build one very large final assembly plant than two or more
smaller ones. Further, moving assembly line techniques have
released this stage of the industry from skilled labour requirements.
On the other hand moving an assembled vehicle over long distances has been very expensive, and substantial savings could be
made by moving the vehicle in 'knocked-down' state to the
market. A single railway wagon that could take only four assembled cars could take about twelve in knocked-down condition.[21] The obvious attractions of this economy have been
further enhanced by the practice in USA of charging the customer
as if the *assembled* car had been transported. Thus, since the war
new assembly plants have been established in widely separated
locations, such as in California, Georgia, Texas, New Jersey and
Massachusetts. (See Fig 3.) This in turn may attract the manu-

facture of some of the parts, tyres for example, near the regional
assembly plant, and this process could eventually make substantial inroads into the strong Detroit regional concentration.[22]
A further feature encouraging dispersal has been the labour
difficulties in the old centre, which are discussed below.

The pull of the market is also evident in the location of the
industry in the UK. Internally, the largest market is in the London
region, but large sales also occur in the south-east region, the west
Midlands, the west Riding of Yorkshire and south Lancashire.
Elsewhere, sales are relatively small, and the Midlands (broadly
defined) remain the best area for access to the internal market.
Further, many thousands of vehicles are marketed overseas, and
closeness to the ports of London and Liverpool enhances the
value of Midlands locations. It is notable that the major car
producers in the country, recently denied by the government their
desire to expand *in situ*, have in the main preferred locations near
Liverpool, where access to materials and components remains
easy and port facilities are close by.

The attractions of a market location for the final assembly stage
are also illustrated by the establishment of assembly plants in
foreign markets, though here the market attraction is usually
enhanced by government activity of some sort. British manufacturers have established assembly plants in Holland, Belgium
and elsewhere, and thereby not only save on freightage but also
benefit from lower import duties on parts than on finished vehicles.
Canadian branches of American firms similarly benefit in both
ways, and numerous other examples could be given.

(d) Factors of production

The importance of the entrepreneur in the location of this
industry has been so often stressed, and so often used, errone-
ously, to demonstrate that location is fortuitous, that we will
discuss this factor first.

The great leaders of this industry have indeed figured promin-
ently in its location. The fact that Ford, Olds, Haynes, Duryea
and others lived in Michigan 'undoubtedly had much to do with
the state of Michigan, and particularly Detroit, becoming the
cradle of auto manufacturing'.[23] In our own country 'Lord Nuffield
selected Cowley because the school in which his father was educated happened to be for sale'.[24] But while the precise points of
production may have some elements of fortuity about their

selection, there is very little fortuitous about the successful general location in the regional sense. In both these areas—southern Michigan, USA, and Oxford, on the borders of the English Midlands—the conditions making for economic and competitive production were good. Had Ford been born in Pueblo, Colorado, and Nuffield's father educated in a school (for sale) in Inverness, it is inconceivable that these admirable motives would have caused them to set up their works in those places. Whatever the location of such fortuitous events as birth, these men, or others, would have commenced operations in the same general areas as have since proved most suited to motor vehicle production. Subsequently, competitive selection would have ensured that the same areas dominated the industry. Other famous men in the American motor industry in fact located initially elsewhere, but the locations of their first choice did not thrive as did that in the lower Michigan area.

The influence of business management on this industry has been profound, attracting, as it did, men of the highest organisational and technical ability. But they have affected location only as to the precise points of production within generally suitable regions. In explaining the enormous concentration at Detroit, for example, we may well need to think in terms of management. Some writers place great stress on this. J. B. Rae, for example, insists that Detroit owed its success to the possession of 'a unique group of individuals with both business and technical ability . . . interested in the . . . motor vehicle'.[25] But the influence of economic and geographic forces was vital in providing a generally favourable environment here, in a broad area within which almost any centre of production would have thrived, given good management. As it happened, Detroit got the best.

Labour requirements have also played a part in forming the geographical pattern of production. But skilled labour, especially in the early years, was usually found along with the supply of materials and components. Workers skilled in metal pressing and shaping, in the manufacture of non-ferrous parts, springs, leather, rubber, engine, electrical and other components were an integral part of the attraction to existing multi-industry areas. Mass-production techniques, however, increased the demand for less skilled labour for assembly line work, until at the present time probably some two-thirds of the labour force of the American motor vehicle industry is of the relatively unskilled kind.[26] This gave the industry greater freedom in locating final assembly plant, but the manufacture of parts and components has not yet matched assembly in mass-production methods and still requires much skilled and semi-skilled labour.

Skilled labour in the UK played a bigger part for a longer period, mainly because cars remained a much more individual product, and the adoption of interchangeability of parts and the moving assembly line came later than in USA.[27] Skilled labour requirements were nevertheless steadily reduced in various ways (for example, spraying with quick-drying paint replaced hand painting in the 1920's), so that labour productivity grew and labour skill requirements fell. With a decreasing need for labour skill, the industry became less tied to locations in Birmingham and Coventry, and in fact a location with unskilled and unorganised labour became a positive advantage for the assembly stage. Once mass-production techniques had taken hold in the UK, 'the most important location force was probably the availability of a large supply of unskilled male labour which could easily be trained [for] operations on the assembly belt'. Birmingham's skilled labour was, if anything, 'a deterrent to the expanding *assembler* of motor cars'.[28] Thus the industry grew at Oxford, Luton and Dagenham, where unskilled labour was available, but still within easy reach of the components suppliers of the west Midlands.

The gradual displacement of labour skills has therefore permitted a greater degree of geographical dispersal, and has assisted the industry to take advantage, especially at the assembly stage, of the economies of a location close to its markets. Another labour consideration is having some influence here: labour attitudes and the generally poor labour-management relations that typify many motor vehicle firms. By its very nature the industry is particularly vulnerable to strikes, for a minor dispute involving a few workers in an outside firm with a near monopoly of the supply of a particular component can bring the whole industry to a standstill. Thus labour costs tend to be increased in the older motor vehicle centres by strikes, stoppages and other union activities, and this encourages a policy of dispersal. Actual wages paid in newer locations may not differ appreciably from those in the main centre, but if attitudes are more favourable and the workers are more ready to accept labour-saving machines, lower labour costs can be obtained. This is well illustrated in USA where Hurley notes a real decentralizing influence at work and a conscious effort by management to build up more harmonious labour relations in new areas.[29]

Capital requirements in this industry are now so large that the entry of a new firm into the industry has become very difficult, if not impossible. Nevertheless, apart from making the industry loth to start operations in an unpromising location, the effects of capital requirements on location have probably been small. Recently, however, government loans on favourable terms have formed part of the inducement to motor vehicle firms in the UK to locate in areas of high unemployment. Discussion of this element is taken up in the next section.

(e) Government

Government intervention in the location of this industry is both direct and indirect. Indirectly, for example, the application of high tariffs on the import of completed vehicles has brought about, as noted above, the location of an increased number of assembly plants in foreign markets. This may even prove to be the first stage in the transferring of the complete production of motors to the protected area. In Australia, for example, government action in 1917 required that two-thirds of all cars were to be imported without bodies. This necessitated the establishment of body-building capacity. Three years later the industry was given tariff protection, and motor vehicle assembly made pronounced growth. After the second world war 'vehicles comprising mainly Australian-made parts began to be produced. Since then, the . . . industry [mainly American and UK manufacturers] . . . has expanded rapidly with government encouragement'.[30]

In the USA the National Industrial Dispersion Programme was drawn up by the government in 1951 to serve strategic requirements. Industry generally was given tax incentives to locate new plants outside certain defined target areas, which included Detroit. The motor vehicle industry has therefore had an added incentive to industrial dispersal.[31]

In the UK past government legislation (for example, the Red Flag legislation) had considerable effects on the growth of the industry, but direct intervention in location has come only in recent years, under the legislation described in Chapter 6. In the late 1950's the motor vehicle industry became anxious to expand its capacity in order to cater for the large increase in demand anticipated in the early 'sixties. Applications for IDCs to permit expansion at, or close by, the existing plants in the midland and southern regions were, however, refused and the industry was subjected to heavy government pressure (both 'stick' and 'carrot' being liberally applied) to expand in areas of economic difficulty. After some bargaining the decision was to permit some expansion in locations of the manufacturers' own first preference (i.e. in the existing major centres) together with a larger, and assisted, expansion in the areas of high unemployment. Naturally enough the most favoured of the permitted areas proved to be that around Merseyside. By locating a new plant here the industry remained close to component manufacturers and material supplies, while the available sites were good and the port of Liverpool was close at hand for exports. Thus, of the 24½ million square feet of new factory space approved by the government for the motor vehicle industry in 1960 and 1961, the North-Western region (i.e. chiefly south Lancashire in this context) received 37 per cent, while the 'traditional' centres received about 33 per cent. The other regions to which the industry had been urged to go were, therefore, less well favoured. Scotland did best, receiving about 12 per cent of the new space, but this location cannot yet be regarded as a favourable one for the mass production of vehicles for a highly competitive market. Since 1963, the government sponsored steel strip mill at Ravenscraig has been in production, which presents some advantage for local vehicle manufacture, but overall both material assembly and final distribution costs are higher here than in traditional centres, while there are other considerable disadvantages for this industry in operating at a location removed from the major centres.[32] Be this as it may, the relevant fact in this context is that, by reason of direct government intervention, the UK motor vehicle industry has recently expanded into new locations.

(f) Other influences

Site requirements are quite important in this industry, since large areas of flat land are required. Ford's Dagenham plant, for example, covers 500 acres. Large land requirements have played a part in the trend of migration from Detroit,[33] where sites are becoming crowded and land expensive. Large quantities of water are also needed (25,000 gallons per hour are used in the sanding section of the paint shop of the Dagenham plant), and much of it must be very pure. Local tax burdens have also influenced location in a small way.[34] There is, however, no room here for a more detailed discussion of the minor influences on location.

Oil refining

Our final example is of another modern and very rapidly expanding industry, petroleum refining.[35] The petroleum industry celebrated its centenary in 1959, but its greatest development has been in the present century, and especially since the first world war. Despite this comparative youthfulness the petroleum refining industry provides a fascinating study of the changing economies of location. While oil wells can be located only where geological conditions permit supplies of oil to exist, refineries can, according to circumstances, be located in widely differing centres and still function effectively and efficiently. Here, then, we may see quite clearly the conflict between the major forces affecting industrial location. On the one hand are the economies to be gained by a location at the material source, and on the other the economies of market proximity or of an 'intermediate' location. In balancing the advantages of each of these three broad types of location, transfer costs (of materials and products) become the most important single economic factor.

As usual, a host of other requirements influence the final location decision, though even in some of these, such as scale of production or pattern of market demand, transfer costs normally play a part. Other influences include labour requirements, patterns of ownership, capital supply and government activity; their role is more important in this industry than in many others because of the geographical location of the raw material, and because of its nature and its consequent processing requirements. But especially one finds in this industry an outstanding illustration of the locational effects of changing technology. Over a comparatively short span of time, remarkable developments have transformed the essential ingredients of location—these developments include changes in the geography of production, in methods of transport, in refining and in the nature and location of the major markets for refinery products. A few illustrations must suffice.

Changes in the geography of production reflect improved techniques of finding and producing oil. Drake's well at Titusville, Pennsylvania, in 1859 struck oil at sixty-nine feet, with the prospector using primitive drilling apparatus designed to drill for water.[36] By pure chance the oil produced was suited, after comparatively simple treatment, to the production of a high proportion of kerosene, for which, almost alone among oil products, there was an immediate market to be developed. Gradually the foundations of oil geology have been laid until, at the present time, a wealth of advanced techniques is applied in the search for oil (even now, however, not always successfully) and large areas containing crude resources have been discovered in various parts of the world. In drilling, the cable tool system by which a hole was pounded out by repeated blows, was replaced in this century by the rotary drill, a tool which is both faster and capable of going much deeper. Before 1924, when cable drilling was still common, the deepest recorded well was 7,350 feet. With the rotary drill, the record moved to 15,000 feet before the second world war, and has since gone to almost 25,000 feet.[37] Such advances, by revolutionising the geography of oil production, have necessarily influenced the pattern of refinery location.

In methods of transport, the barrels taken by horse wagon and barge were replaced in USA in the 1860's by railway tank cars, tank barges and pipelines. It is in particular the great development of pipelines that has been the most significant feature of long distance overland movement of oil and oil products in the present century, enabling crude petroleum to be moved hundreds of miles to market or intermediate refineries, and refined products to be distributed swiftly and cheaply over enormous market areas. For sea transport ocean-going tankers of ever increasing size have been the most potent factor in reducing transport costs of crude oil and making possible the location of refineries in areas far removed from oil resources.

In techniques of refining the simple heating and distillation of the early refineries has been superseded by the exceedingly complex methods of the modern refinery. Each advance in refining techno-logy has had locational implications: for example enabling crude oil of different types, or containing various impurities, to be utilised; or enabling each refinery to suit its output to the particu-lar types of product in demand in the market it is built to serve.

Above all, however, the refining industry has been affected in its location by technical advances that have developed the market for its products. This feature cannot always be readily disentangled from the others. Advance in refining techniques and transport im-provements, for example, contributes directly to the broadening of the market for oil products, but here we are more immediately concerned with the development of markets for a variety of differ-ent oil products and with the effects of such market growth upon refinery location. We shall now give more detailed attention to that aspect.

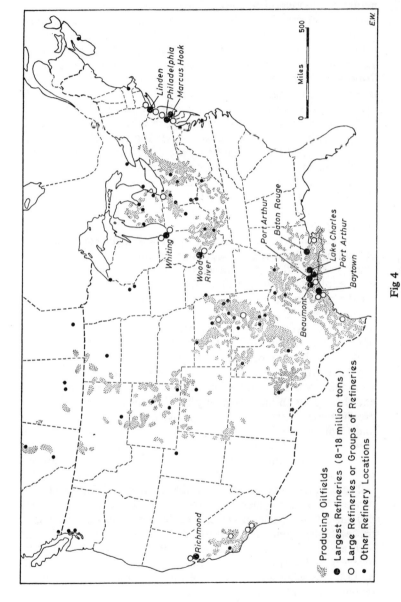

Fig 4

USA Oil refinery locations, *circa 1960*

In the early stages of the growth of the industry, the limited nature of the market encouraged location of refineries at or near the source of the oil. There was a latent demand for an illuminating fuel (kerosene), but no demand existed, or could be readily created, for most of the remaining fractions of the petroleum. These were waste products, and the main problem was how to dispose of them. The marketable yield from the earliest refineries in Pennsylvania, therefore, despite the very favourable nature of the crude oil, did not exceed about 50 per cent of the crude, and the remainder that was not consumed in refinery operation was dumped or burnt.[38] Improvements in refining gradually raised the marketable yield from these light-base oils to about 75 per cent, but the quantity of waste remained an important feature in restricting refineries to locations on the oilfields themselves (especially, for example, around Pittsburgh), or at such other centres (Cleveland, Ohio, for example) as had relatively cheap access to crude supplies.

From about 1870 petroleum became increasingly a major source of lubricants but, vital though this product is in the modern machine civilisation, it has never provided more than a small proportion of total refinery output. By far the most important event for the refining industry came at the turn of the century with the development of the internal combustion engine and the emergence of the motor vehicle. The considerable 'light end' waste product of nineteenth-century refineries rapidly became the major product in the first decades of the twentieth century. This brought new problems. Much larger quantities of crude oil had to be refined to meet this growing demand for 'top end' or 'light end' fractions, and this meant an increasing surplus of the heavier fractions. The problem was accentuated by the greater use of crude oil from the mid-Continent and Gulf fields in USA, which had a heavier base than the Pennsylvanian oils. Other things being equal, the best location for the refinery was still either on, or close to, the centres of oil production.

The problem was eased by the development of the 'cracking' process by which some of the heavier oil was broken down to provide a bigger yield of petrol, but there is a limit to this costly process. The eventual solution was in the development of new markets for the heavier fractions. This began with fuel oil for furnaces and was accentuated, especially after the 1914–18 war, by the increasing use of diesel oils as power sources for ships, locomotives and road vehicles. Both of these markets have continued to expand. Fuel oil in particular, especially since the close of the second world war, has made heavy inroads into markets formerly monopolised by coal, such as steel-works, glass works and power stations. On the other hand the development of jet and turbo-jet aircraft has once more increased the market for kerosene. When we recall that the growing petroleum-chemical industry can utilise many residual refinery products, it becomes clear that the modern refinery faces a market demand for almost everything it can produce. Saleable products are derived from between 90 and 95 per cent of the crude oil received—and about half of the small non-saleable proportion is, in fact, fuel utilised by the refinery itself in its operation.

In such circumstances market location has become more attractive. Over a twenty-year period (1939–59) when world refining capacity (excluding communist countries) increased four-fold, the proportion of resource-oriented capacity fell from about 70 per cent to 35 per cent, while market-oriented capacity rose from about 30 per cent to 56 per cent. The residual 9 per cent in 1959 was accounted for by intermediate locations.[39]

While market-oriented refining capacity has grown in the world's largest single refining country, USA, the most significant and interesting growth has been that in western Europe.* This has been made possible by the enormous post-war growth in demand for oil products in western European countries, and by the fact that the structure of this demand has been broadly such as to permit the absorption of the full range of modern refinery products. Before the war only USA possessed a sufficiently large and well-balanced demand to enable refinery production in market locations to be economic. Other markets, including those in western Europe, were best supplied with their own particular needs of refined products from large refineries located near their oil supply. This avoided transfer costs on unwanted materials. For such reasons, USA overwhelmingly dominated world refining capacity in 1938, possessing about 70 per cent of the total. Most of the rest was to be found in the Caribbean, the Middle East and the East Indies, i.e. at the oil source. Western Europe possessed only 4 per cent of world refining capacity in 1938.[40]

This situation has now changed. Not only has there been a great expansion of demand, outside USA, for a wide range of refinery products, but the development of the super-tanker has made it far more economic to ship enormous quantities of crude oil over

* And, more recently, in Japan.

long distances to market refineries than to ship smaller loads of different products. The market refinery economises greatly in the costs of distributing its final products, and this has become an increasingly important consideration as the number and variety of end products of refineries has grown.

Further elements in the great expansion of refining capacity at market as opposed to resource locations (and especially in those market areas that are without important indigenous petroleum reserves) are the high capital cost of a modern refinery and the changed geography of crude oil supplies. The modern refinery gains considerable economies from large-scale operation. Up to a point, the larger the output, the lower the capital cost per unit of product. Within certain limits 'doubling the size of a prospective plant will increase investment cost by only about 60 per cent'.[41] In addition, the operating costs in a large refinery are lower per unit of output than in a smaller one. Thus the large refinery is now becoming the rule in all countries with sufficient demand. But the size of the modern refinery is reflected in high capital costs. The existing UK refinery at Fawley, with a capacity (1965) of 11·5 million tons, is said to represent an investment of about £90 million.[42] The investment of such a sum will not be undertaken casually, and the huge capital requirements have implications which tend to favour market area locations.

In general, for example, the necessary capital is not available in the under-developed countries of the Middle East, from which most of western Europe's crude oil is now drawn, and the choice of refinery location normally rests with large oil companies whose origins are in north-west Europe and North America. From the point of view of the capital investment alone, it is unlikely that a location for a new refinery to serve western Europe would be preferred in one of these areas of crude oil supply. Actual running costs may vary little as between developed and under-developed areas, but investment costs (and therefore total operating costs) are likely to be considerably higher in new under-developed area locations. Houses, transport services, water and electricity supplies will probably be required in addition to the refinery plant itself. Such supplies and services already exist in the major market areas.

From the point of view of initial capital requirements, therefore, the balance of advantage lies, in such a situation, with the market location. But there are additional features of importance, especially for western Europe, that enhance the attractions of market refineries as compared with those of resource-oriented refineries in under-developed areas of oil supply. It is not always that one can say with certainty that investment in these source areas is secure. Political instability is a strong incentive to locate refineries away from under-developed regions, and the crisis in 1951, when the Persian government expropriated the great Abadan refinery, was followed by a renewed expansion of refinery capacity in western Europe. An extremely highly capitalised industry such as this cannot afford the long idle periods which may be imposed by adverse political conditions. Idleness, however, may be the least unattractive prospect. The resource-based refinery in under-developed areas is particularly vulnerable to local disturbances, and even, as at Abadan, to expropriation. Further, the resource refinery is for all practical purposes tied to its one source of supply. The market refinery in western Europe and elsewhere has greater flexibility in obtaining crude supplies economically. In times of difficulty (as, for example, during the Middle East crisis of 1956) it can draw oil supplies from other producing areas. It would have been a far graver situation in 1956–7 if the oil companies serving the western European market had had most, or even a large part, of their total refining capacity located in the Middle East.

A further attraction of a market location in western Europe has been the availability of skilled engineers and technicians. It is true that labour costs form a low proportion of total costs in a modern refinery—possibly under 10 per cent[43]—but the small labour requirement contains a large proportion of highly skilled personnel. It is normally easier and cheaper to recruit such essential labour for a home refinery than for an overseas location at the source of the crude oil.

For a variety of reasons, governments in western Europe have also encouraged the development of substantial refining capacity within their own countries. Many governments here, and elsewhere, apply preferential tariffs that favour imports of crude oil as against refined products. In the UK in the late 1940's the government permitted the necessary capital to be allocated to building up refining capacity during a period of severe capital shortage, and with a large number of other essential projects on hand.[44] The reasons for such government intervention included the desire to conserve foreign exchange in a period of stringency, and to offset serious internal fuel supply deficiencies in western Europe by increased imports of oil. The import of huge quantities of crude petroleum in large tankers is very much cheaper than the purchase from overseas of separate cargoes of many different petroleum products. Not only can it save foreign exchange and transfer costs, but the domestic refinery industry can also provide the basis of a useful export trade. For the UK, for example, the export of oil products nowadays earns more foreign currency than the traditional export of coal. In addition, native refining capacity provides the basis of development for the important petro-chemical industry. Apart from balance of payments considerations, political and strategic reasoning also lies behind government support of rapid refinery expansion in western Europe since the war.

Government activity in this context, however, has not been restricted to western Europe or to market locations. In some instances refineries are located in oil source locations under pressure from the government concerned, or by agreement prior to the discovery or oil. Thus, when in 1958 a Japanese oil consortium applied for permission to seek and exploit oil reserves in Saudi Arabia, the final agreement stipulated that, should oil be discovered, and extraction reach a rate of $1\frac{1}{2}$ million tons per annum for ninety days, a refinery be built in Saudi Arabia. With further expansion of crude production to an annual rate of $3\frac{3}{4}$ million tons the capacity of the refinery would have to be raised to not less than 30 per cent of the crude output. The refinery would have to produce the whole range of end products and contain plant to use natural gas for petroleum chemical manufacture.[45] Whether or not such an agreement would be pushed through to completion will naturally depend very much upon the general conditions of petroleum supply in the world as a whole. A more concrete example of this type of government influence can be taken from Venezuela. Before the war Venezuela's refinery capacity amounted to only 4 million tons, while her crude oil production amounted to about 28 million tons. The Hydrocarbons Act of 1943 was directed at persuading the oil companies concerned to construct additional refining capacity. Venezuela's refining capacity now amounts to some 50 million tons (Table 13), and part at least of this expansion reflects the success of the 1943 Act.

Nevertheless, the most remarkable change in refinery location since 1945 has been in the growth of capacity in western Europe. The 4 per cent of total world refining capacity that existed here in 1938 had risen to 20 per cent by 1963—and this of a total world capacity (1,508 million tons) some four times as large as in 1938. One further important consideration in this expansion must now

TABLE 13

WORLD OIL PRODUCTION AND REFINING CAPACITY, 1963

	Production '000 metric tons	(%)	Refining '000 metric tons capacity	(%)
USA	410,270	30·44	509,420	33·79
Canada	37,430	2·11	31,365	3·41
Mexico	17,000	1·32	18,750	1·24
West Indies	6,290	0·51	26,535	1·76
South America	202,830	14·95	150,410	10·04
of which				
Venezuela	(169,570)	(12·58)	(50,505)	(3·36)
Western Europe	18,880	1·40	299,580	19·87
of which				
UK	(120)	(0·01)	(56,160)	(3·72)
France	(3,040)	(0·25)	(51,600)	(3·42)
Italy	(1,790)	(0·13)	(57,985)	(3·84)
West Germany	(7,530)	(0·55)	(61,735)	(4·10)
Netherlands	(2,200)	(0·16)	(26,705)	(1·77)
Eastern Europe, USSR and China	227,620	16·89	230,500	15·30
of which				
USSR	(206,100)	(15·29)	(195,000)	(12·94)
Rumania	(12,230)	(0·91)	(13,000)	(0·86)
China (incl. oil shale)	(6,000)	(0·45)	(8,000)	(0·53)
Middle East	344,720	25·57	97,135	6·44
of which				
Kuwait	(97,200)	(7·22)	(17,125)	(1·14)
Saudi Arabia	(81,140)	(6·02)	(11,800)	(0·78)
Iran	(72,830)	(5·40)	(25,105)	(1·67)
Iraq	(56,670)	(4·20)		
Kuwait/Saudi Arabia neutral zone	(16,440)	(1·22)		
Egypt	(5,720)	(0·42)	(7,650)	(0·51)
Far East and Australasia	30,360	2·25	123,935	8·22
of which				
Indonesia	(23,160)	(1·72)	(13,910)	(0·92)
Japan	(810)	(0·06)	(68,405)	(4·54)
Africa (excl. Egypt)	51,280	3·80	17,620	1·17
Algeria	(23,340)	(1·73)		
Libya	(22,130)	(1·64)		
World Total	1,348,100		1,507,500	

Source: Petroleum Information Bureau

be mentioned—the changed structure of demand for oil products in western Europe. This was just as necessary as an increase of total demand if large modern refineries were to be located economically in this region. If the market cannot absorb the full range of refinery products there are three possible courses of action. The first, and often most economical, is to import the necessary refined petroleum products. The second is to construct smaller refineries (thus foregoing important economies of scale) to meet part of the demand, and to import deficient items. The third is to build efficient, large, plant and export the surplus products. This necessitates the finding of a suitable foreign market and involves extra transfer costs in back-hauling or cross-hauling refinery products.

In western Europe before the war, demand was concentrated, unfavourably for economic refinery operation, on the lighter fractions. In the UK, for example, in 1938 the demand for petrol amounted to 56 per cent of total petroleum product demand, and kerosene accounted for a further 8 per cent. This may be compared with an approximate 'natural' yield of Middle East crude oil of 20 to 22 per cent petrol. Even by installing substantial, and very expensive, cracking plant, the petrol yield could be raised only a few per cent. Thus the inadequate balance of demand was a severe handicap to economic operation of refineries in the UK before the war, and native refineries therefore provided only one-fifth of total petroleum product demand.

Since the war, however, there has been a very large increase in the consumption of the heavier petroleum products in western Europe. Demand for petrol has risen, but much more slowly than that for diesel and fuel oils, for which transport and industrial demand has been high and progressively increasing. Table 14 shows how substantially the structure of demand in European countries has changed in post-war years. Up to a point the more rapidly growing demand for the heavier fractions eased the refiners' problems, bringing demand somewhat more closely into line with the 'natural' yield of Middle East crudes (i.e. about 20–22 per cent petrol; 18–20 per cent gas-diesel oils; 43–45 per cent residual fuel oils).[46] But a problem then arose of an opposite kind to that of the pre-war years—a surplus of petrol, which led to a period of severe competition between companies in several European countries. This problem, however, is in turn being countered by the rapidly growing use of naphtha (light end fractions) in the production of town gas.

TABLE 14

STRUCTURE OF DEMAND FOR PETROLEUM PRODUCTS

Western Europe and selected countries, 1950 and 1963

	Gasoline		Kerosene		Gas/diesel oil		Fuel oil		Other*		Total (million tons)	
	1950	1963	1950	1963	1950	1963	1950	1963	1950	1963	1950	1963
	(per cent)		(per cent)		(per cent)		(per cent)		(per cent)			
United Kingdom	35·6	17·4	9·3	3·6	17·9	16·9	21·2	43·8	15·8	18·3	14·8	52·6
France	27·1	19·4	1·2	0·4	23·9	39·9	36·5	24·0	11·3	16·3	9·2	36·2
West Germany	29·8	16·0	7·2	0·1	30·2	45·7	12·0	24·4	20·8	13·8	3·4	52·8
Italy	15·6	14·1	4·3	0·8	17·7	11·6	54·0	59·5	8·4	14·0	4·2	32·6
Western Europe	28·0	15·8	5·7	2·0	21·2	30·3	31·8	37·4	13·3	14·5	49·0	252·7

Source: Petroleum Press Service

* Including aviation fuels, bitumen, lubricants and other products

Most of the changes in refinery location that have occurred in recent years are bound up broadly with the kinds of development in oil production and utilisation that have been described. In detail of course (as the foregoing may illustrate) the matter can become highly complex, but the various issues cannot be followed through in detail here.[47] Among other considerations reflected in location are the pattern of ownership in the industry, pricing and marketing policies, and the requirements of site. Of the former influence we may merely note here that eight major companies (five American and three European) control most of the crude oil production, most of the means of transport, and most of the refining capacity in the world. Any policy that these companies adopt is bound to influence the world pattern of this industry. It has been considered that this ownership pattern affects location by 'modifying the economic consequences of geography',[48] especially through the operation of a pricing system that links the price of crude oil in the Middle East with that in the USA, and the prices of ex-refinery products in Europe to those for similar products in the USA. With such a degree of government interest in refinery location as now exists, however, the consequences of this practice should not be overstressed.

The precise pattern of refinery location is, however, strongly affected by site requirements. The modern refinery covers a large area of land, and the plant needs a suitable geological foundation. In addition, there must be adequate provision for bringing huge quantities of crude oil economically to the site. In most present market locations this means deep water close to the shore. All sites, everywhere, must be able to provide the refinery with enormous quantities of water at low cost.[49] These requirements have been reflected in new refinery construction in western Europe since the war, which has been chiefly at coastal sites. Of late, however, there have been new developments on the continent, with the aim of getting much closer to the final consumer than a coastal site will allow. In western Germany, for example, the Hamburg and Bremen refineries are considerably removed from the largest, and most rapidly growing, centres of demand, which are in the Rhine-Ruhr area and in southern Germany. Now, however, such is the total demand in these areas that pipelines have been, and are being, laid to supply their own refineries with crude oil. Ruhr refineries are now supplied with crude oil by pipes from Wilhelmshaven and Rotterdam. New refineries have been built at Karlsruhe and Strasbourg, supplied by pipeline from Marseilles,[50] and there have been important developments at Ingoldstadt in Bavaria, served by extensions of the pipeline from Karlsruhe.

The major change in the pattern of refinery location since the war, therefore, has been the growth of capacity in countries with a large demand but little, if any, crude oil. But in the general world expansion of refining (370 million tons capacity in 1938, 1,508 million tons in 1963) all types of location have increased their capacity, with the resource-oriented refinery, however, losing ground to the even more rapidly expanding market-oriented refineries. The USA, though less dominant than before the war, remains a giant in the field of oil production, refining and consumption. (See Table 13.) It is in that country perhaps that purely economic considerations have their fullest play in refinery location, but comparisons with other countries are not very useful since the non-communist world possesses no other similar example of a country with both huge resources and a huge demand. The present pattern of refinery location in USA is shown on the map (Fig 4). There are some 300 refineries in all, but many of these are old and small, and a large proportion of total capacity is provided by the relatively few refineries of great size. The USA provides examples of locations oriented to crude supplies and to markets, and of locations at intermediate points. Here, as elsewhere, the attractions of a market location have increased, and this has been given added impetus by the rise in demand for heavier fractions. The piping of heavy fuel oils from source refineries to a market a thousand miles or more away is difficult and expensive, and this consideration adds to the other attractions of a location near the main markets.

Further large expansion of world refinery capacity is in prospect, and much of it will continue to be in western Europe. The expansion of output from existing sites provides substantial economies, but the selection of entirely new locations for refining capacity (as now in inland sites in western Europe) indicates that the pattern of refinery location has not yet become a stable one. A further aspect of planned refinery construction is to be seen also in the establishment of refineries in smaller consuming areas, as in the Far East, Africa and Latin America. Whether this is, or will become, economically justifiable is another matter.[51]

We find, then, in this industry an important change in the overall pattern of location in the last two decades. In the first forty years of the twentieth century there had developed a marked dominance of oil-source refineries. The pattern now emerging, however, promises an increasing dominance of market-oriented refineries. This remarkable change has been conditioned by technological developments in crude oil production, in refining and, most of all, in the use of oil products.

[1] See the *Guardian*, 19 February 1960

[2] J. B. Rae, *American Automobile Manufacturers*, 1959, p. 19

[3] Ibid., p. 45

[4] *Structure of Competitive Industry*, 1953, p. 152

[5] See Rae, op. cit., chapter 5

[6] Ibid., p. 58

[7] Ibid., pp. 119 and 153

[8] 'Political and Economic Planning', *Motor Vehicles*, 1950, p. 5

[9] Rae, op. cit., pp. 173 and 192

[10] *Economist*, 29 August 1959, p. 655

[11] Ibid., p. 657

[12] Ibid., p. 655

[13] P.E.P., op. cit., pp. 5–6

[14] G. C. Allen, *British Industries and their Organization*, 3rd ed., 1952, p. 167

[15] Rae, op. cit., p. 202

[16] Allen, op. cit., p. 171

[17] Morris and Austin, for example, joined to form the BMC.; while Standard and Triumph also joined forces, but have since been absorbed by the Leyland group, whose chief interest lies in commercial vehicle manufacture.

[18] Rae, op. cit., p. 59

[19] Allen, op. cit., 4th ed., 1959, p. 176

[20] N. P. Hurley, 'The Automotive Industry. A Study in Location', *Land Economics*, February 1959, p. 2.

[21] Ibid., p. 5

[22] Ibid., p. 12. It is worth noting, however, that the development of new types of railway rolling stock is now enabling the US railway companies to transport *assembled* vehicles at highly competitive rates. This may well slow down the process of decentralisation. See *Fortune*, July 1965, p. 132

[23] Ibid., p. 1

[24] Robinson, op. cit., p. 152

[25] Rae, op. cit., p. 59

[26] Hurley, op. cit., p. 7

[27] Allen, op. cit., 4th ed., p. 190

[28] M. Beesley, 'Changing Locational Advantages in the British Motor Car Industry', *Journal of Industrial Economics*, vol. VI, 1957–8, pp. 50–1. (Our italics)

[29] Hurley, op. cit., p. 8

[30] P. Scott, The Australian Motor Vehicle Industry', *Geography*, July 1959, p. 209

[31] Hurley, op. cit., p. 13

[32] See R. C. Estall, 'New Locations in Motor Vehicle Manufacture', *Town and Country Planning*, March 1964

[33] Hurley, op. cit., p. 11

[34] Ibid., p. 8, fn. 41

[35] An important new study of this industry is *An Economic Geography of Oil*, P. R. Odell, 1963. Refinery location is examined at some length

[36] P. H. Giddens, *The Birth of the Oil Industry*, 1938, p. 19

[37] Shell Petroleum Company Ltd., *The Petroleum Handbook*, 1959, p. 77

[38] Giddens, op. cit., p. 92

[39] 'Economic Factors in Refinery Location', *Petroleum Press Service*, July 1959, p. 249

[40] *Petroleum Handbook*, op. cit., p. 13

[41] *Petroleum Press Service*, op. cit., p. 250

[42] It is of further significance in location (cf. iron and steel) that a proposal to raise this capacity to 16·5 million tons suggests that only £7 million of additional capital would be required

[43] C. A. Heller in United Nations: Department of Economic and Social Affairs, *Techniques of Petroleum Development*. NY 1964, p. 193 ff.

[44] White Paper, *CMD 7268*, 1948

[45] *Economist*, 17 May 1958

[46] A. Melamid, 'Geographical Distribution of Petroleum Refining Capacities', *Economic Geography*, 1955, p. 170. But the new Saharan oils are very much lighter and their increasing use may bring new problems

[47] The study by P. R. Odell, op. cit., dwells at greater length on these complexities

[48] United Nations: Economic Commission for Europe, op. cit., p. 6

[49] The siting of B.P. refineries is described by H. Longhurst, *Adventure in Oil* 1952, Chap. 16

[50] See T. H. Elkins, 'Oil in Germany', *Geography*, 1960

[51] Petroleum Press Service, June 1964 and August 1965

Reading in location theory
Many valuable books and articles have been mentioned in footnotes. Students requiring more advanced reading are referred to:

E. M. Hoover, *The Location of Economic Activity*, 1948
A. Weber, *The Location of Industry* (trans. Friederich), 1929, reissued 1957
A. Losch, *The Economics of Location*, 1954
W. Isard, *Location and Space Economy*, 1956
M. L. Greenhut, *Plant Location in Theory and Practice*, 1956
P. Haggett, *Locational Analysis in Human Geography*, 1965.

CONCLUSION

It is hoped that these three brief studies of the location requirements of industries have helped to illustrate the significance in
practice of the many influences discussed in the body of the book.
In these industries, it must surely be clear, location is not, and
never has been, a matter of indifference, and the same claim may
reasonably be made for industries in general. It is possible that not
many location choices are bad enough to cause an almost immediate and complete collapse of an enterprise (though this has been
known), but *all* industries are affected in their profitability and in
their consequent capacity for growth by their location. There is in
fact no industry whose prospects are not appreciably improved
by a good location, or materially worsened by a poor one. To
assist in the assessment of locational values and qualities is an
important part of the economic geographer's contribution to
industry and to society.

INDEX